OVER LAKELAND MOUNTAINS

25 Walks across the 71 Major Summits

Bleaberry Combe and Crummock Water from High Stile

OVER LAKELAND MOUNTAINS

25 Walks across the
71 Major Summits

by

Paul Hannon

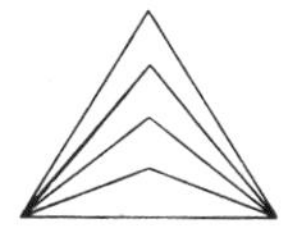

HILLSIDE PUBLICATIONS

HILLSIDE PUBLICATIONS
11 Nessfield Grove
Exley Head
Keighley
West Yorkshire
BD22 6NU

ISBN 1 870141 08 3

Printed in Great Britain by
Carnmor Print and Design
95/97 London Road
Preston
Lancashire
PR1 4BA

CONTENTS

INTRODUCTION

This book is a practical guide to 25 circular routes that between them encompass the 71 major mountains of the Lake District National Park. The vast majority of the walks take in two or more mountains, and in most cases can be expected to occupy the best part of a full day on the hills. The routes have been planned in order to incorporate their chosen mountains in a logical manner, so as neither to climb to the tops and then have to return immediately to the valley, nor to simply attempt to 'bag' as many tops as possible in a single outing.

While even the most demanding of these walks should be within the capabilities of the average fellwalker, it would be most unwise to recommend them to the inexperienced. As there is only one way to acquire such experience, novice mountain walkers are best advised to acquaint themselves with shorter walks over lower fells, preferably in settled weather conditions, then move on with confidence to the dizzy heights over 2000 feet. Mountain safety is a subject dealt with in many a chunky volume, and here it should be sufficient to say that the most important elements are to be properly equipped, realistically aware of limitations such as time and physical condition, and be as at home with a map and compass as with a guidebook.

Although the purpose of the guide is to supply sufficient details of the routes, the accompanying maps serve only to portray them, with the role of supporting the relevant Ordnance Survey map. Mountain Lakeland is admirably served by four Outdoor Leisure maps at the 1:25,000 scale, which ideally depict the complicated and tightly packed mountain features of the district. Only one further map at this scale is needed to give complete coverage of the walks described. A useful tip is to mark the route on the map in thick pencil beforehand.

At the start of each walk description, an information box supplies details of the distance, amount of climbing, and the time to allow. The time scale ranges from Naismith's formula of 3mph plus a half-hour for every thousand feet of ascent, to a very generous extreme of fifty percent longer: the nature of the terrain has also been taken into account. The starting point is listed along with a grid reference for the less obvious ones.

The magic altitude of 2000 feet has been retained for conferring mountain status, despite the fact that metric maps have long since replaced the trusty imperial sheets. Accepting that improved surveying methods have brought about many amendments to summit heights, the metric figures have been used, and conversions to our traditional feet also included. An attempt to define separate mountains has been made in a similar fashion to the principle set out by George Bridge in his industrious *The Mountains of England and Wales* (1973), though with slight variations. To qualify as independent, a mountain requires a minimum amount of re-ascent from the highest saddle with the nearest superior mountain, this minimum receding with distance. A subsidiary top is one that fails to meet the above criteria, but manages to lift itself at least 50 feet above any col.

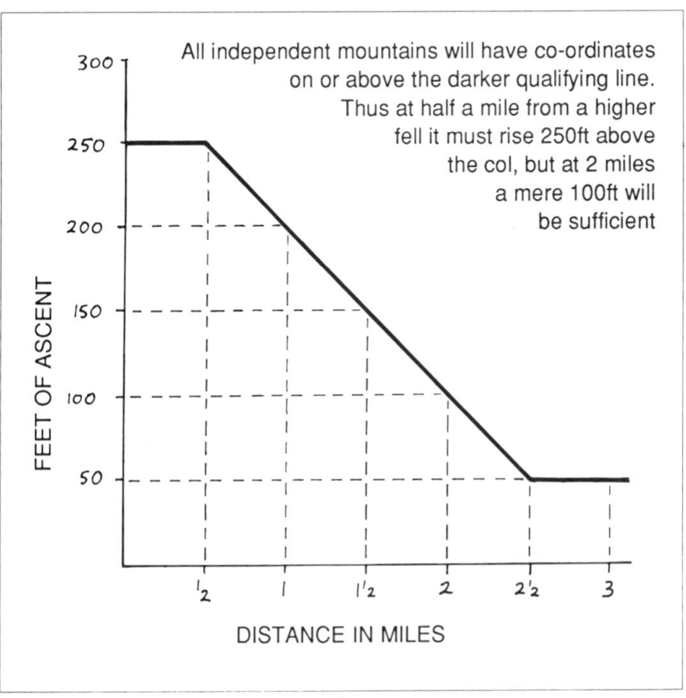

Improved mapping combined with a reassessment of suspect entries has resulted in numerous differences to Bridge's list, and a net loss of three mountains has been recorded.

It is hoped that the listing is found to be useful by the enthusiast: it should prove as accurate as is practicable, although inevitably certain inclusions and omissions must be border-line cases. The the complete table of mountains is given on pages 10 and 11.

Accepting it is tidy, and to many, essential to have an up-to-date table such as this, at the end of the day there can be no mountain not worth a walk over. Lakeland in particular has so many fells that could only ever be described as shoulders of higher tops, but still remain essential components of the mountain scene: the two Red Pikes, for example, are of no less merit simply because they are only a short pull from near-neighbours High Stile and Scoat Fell.

A sizeable number of these subsidiary tops have inevitably, by their very locations, found their way into the walks described, and indeed make highly valuable contributions to their walks. At the start of each walk they have therefore been listed in a manner appropriate to their subservience. To conclude, it is worth remembering that in many way these walks only scratch the surface, for still above the 2000 foot line there are countless wonderful places to be: ridges alone include Causey Pike, Whiteside, Ullock Pike, and the one and only Striding Edge.

Finally, the overwhelming popularity of these wonderful hills is only too evident to all who visit them, and the thinking walker can best show respect for our fragile paths by faithfully following zig-zags and avoiding insensitive shortcuts, not descending at speed, not walking the hills in enormous groups, and wearing less hefty footwear whenever possible.

THE WALKS

An outline map of the Lake District, showing the location of each starting point in relation to the major lakes and roads

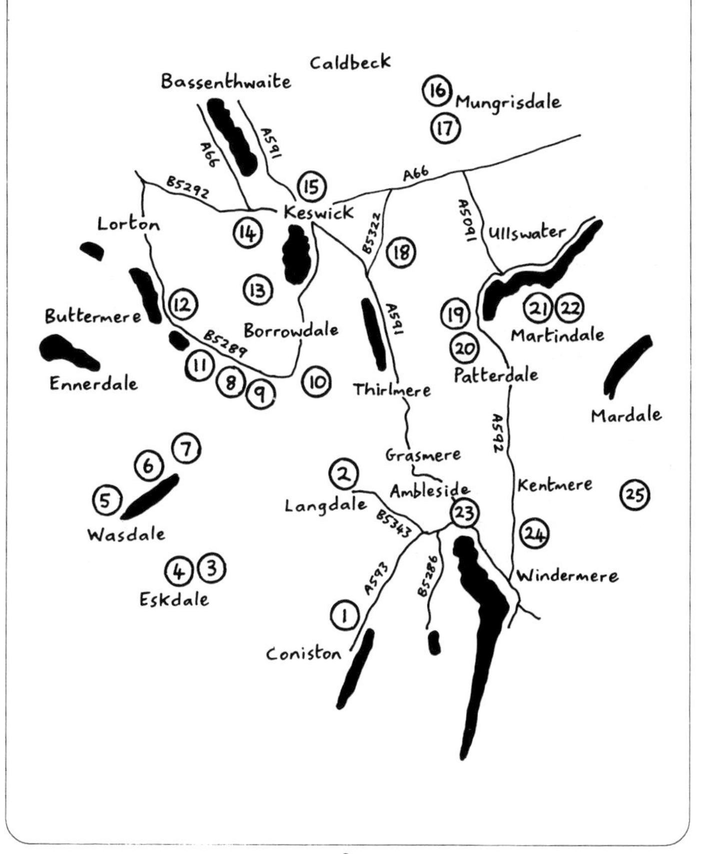

THE LAKE DISTRICT MOUNTAINS

	MOUNTAIN	METRES	FEET	WALK NO.
1	Scafell Pike	978	3208	7
2	Scafell	964	3162	7
3	Helvellyn	950	3116	19
4	Skiddaw	931	3054	15
5	Great End	910	2984	9
6	Bowfell	902	2960	3
7	Great Gable	899	2949	8
8	Pillar	892	2927	6
9	Catstycam	890	2919	19
10	Esk Pike	885	2903	3
11	Raise	883	2896	19
12	Fairfield	873	2863	23
13	Blencathra	868	2847	17
14	Crinkle Crags	859	2818	3
15	Dollywaggon Pike	858	2814	20
16	Great Dodd	857	2811	18
17	Grasmoor	852	2795	14
18	Stybarrow Dodd	843	2765	18
19	Saint Sunday Crag	841	2758	20
20	Scoat Fell	841	2758	6
21	Eel Crag	839	2752	14
22	High Street	828	2716	22
23	High Stile	807	2647	12
24	Coniston Old Man	803	2634	1
25	High Raise (Martindale)	802	2631	22
26	Kirk Fell	802	2631	8
27	Swirl How	802	2631	1
28	Lingmell	800+	2624+	7
29	Haycock	797	2614	5
30	Dove Crag	792	2598	23
31	Grisedale Pike	791	2594	14
32	Glaramara	783	2568	9
33	Dow Crag	778	2552	1
34	Harter Fell (Mardale)	778	2552	25

	MOUNTAIN	METRES	FEET	WALK NO.
35	Red Screes	776	2545	23
36	Grey Friar	770+	2526+	1
37	Hopegill Head	770	2526	14
38	Caudale Moor	763	2503	24
39	Wetherlam	763	2503	1
40	High Raise (Langstrath)	762	2499	10
41	Ill Bell	757	2483	24
42	Dale Head	753	2470	13
43	Robinson	737	2417	13
44	Harrison Stickle	736	2414	10
45	Seat Sandal	736	2414	20
46	Hindscarth	727	2385	13
47	Clough Head	726	2381	18
48	Ullscarf	726	2381	10
49	Brandreth	715	2345	8
50	Lonscale Fell	715	2345	15
51	Branstree	713	2339	25
52	Knott	710	2329	16
53	Pike o'Blisco	705	2312	2
54	Bowscale Fell	702	2303	17
55	Rest Dodd	696	2283	22
56	Seatallan	692	2270	5
57	Great Calva	690	2263	16
58	Sheffield Pike	675	2214	19
59	Scar Crags	672	2204	14
60	Loadpot Hill	671	2201	22
61	Tarn Crag	664	2178	25
62	Carrock Fell	660+	2165+	16
63	High Pike	658	2158	16
64	Place Fell	657	2155	21
65	Harter Fell (Eskdale)	653	2142	4
66	High Spy	653	2142	13
67	Fleetwith Pike	648	2125	11
68	Iron Crag	640+	2099+	5
69	Starling Dodd	633	2076	12
70	Yewbarrow	628	2060	6
71	Great Borne	616	2020	12

WALK 1 THE CONISTON FELLS

L33	**DOW CRAG**	2552ft/778m
L24	**CONISTON OLD MAN**	2634ft/803m
	Brim Fell	2611ft/796m
L36	**GREY FRIAR**	2526+ft/770+m
	Great Carrs	2558+ft/780+m
L27	**SWIRL HOW**	2631ft/802m
L39	**WETHERLAM**	2503ft/763m

Start: Coniston Map: SW Sheet
14 miles / 4300 feet / 7-10 hours
Parking: large car park in village

Dow Crag

Departure from Coniston is an uninspiring prelude to a day on the tops, for a mile of steep road is needed to gain the open fell. From the bridge by the Black Bull in the village centre, a back road climbs above the beck and up past the Sun Hotel, passing the former station yard before embracing the gradients of a narrowing road that eventually expires at the forever opening and shutting 'Fell Gate.'

Of the two unsurfaced tracks heading away, the route takes that to the left: this is the Walna Scar Road, an exceptionally undemanding climb to the 2000ft contour. Features along the way include the reedy pool of Boo Tarn; a popular path departing right for the Cove and Goat's Water; and the crossing of the outflowing Torver Beck at Cove Bridge. For a while Dow Crag's irrepressible rock face shows itself across the Cove, and as the walk unfolds it will be appreciated from many angles.

On gaining Walna Scar Pass, the old packhorse route is sent on its way down to the Duddon valley, and steps turn to the flank on the right. A good path climbs to a cairn on Brown Pike, with the remarkably circular Blind Tarn below, and the next minor top of Buck Pike ahead. From this point a simple stroll leads along the ridge, the final section to Dow Crag illuminated by striking views down into the gullies high above Goat's Water.

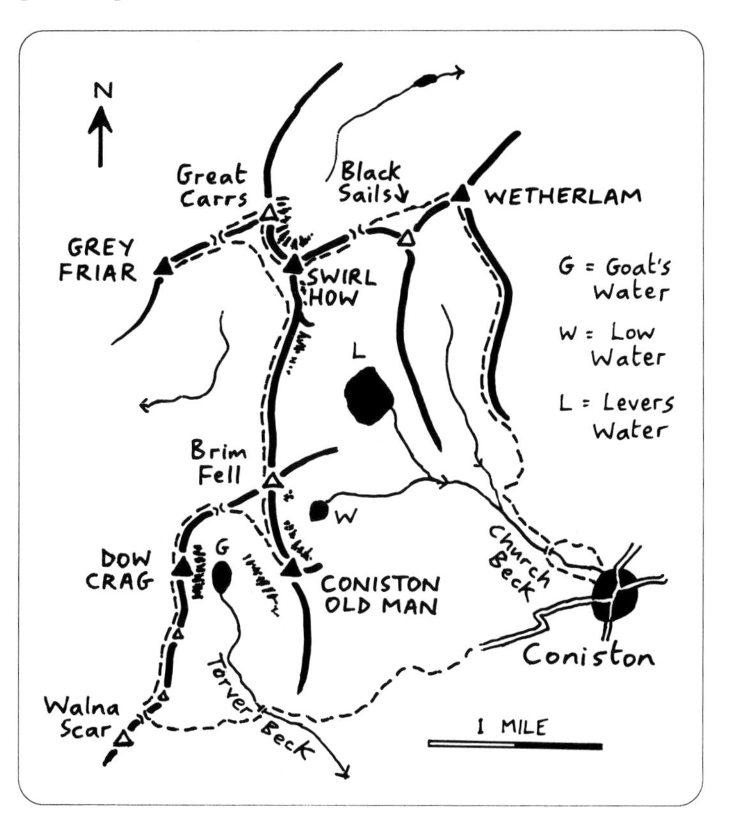

Coniston Old Man

From the naked rock of the summit much of the way ahead can be surveyed, and the next stage to Coniston Old Man, which looms large across the hollow of the tarn, involves a straightforward circuit of the rim of the combe. The descent to Goat's Hause is rapidly accomplished, and the pull onto the Old Man soon brings arrival at the great platform marking the highest point of the walk. It is gained amidst another birds-eye view of a mountain tarn, this time its own Low Water.

Grey Friar

From the Old Man long strides are the order of the day, turning back northwards along the rim of Low Water's combe, with a broad path on excellent turf leading to the solid cairn on Brim Fell. Continuing along the whaleback ridge, the saddle of Levers Hause interrupts the direct climb to Swirl How, and during the descent to it, it is useful to locate a narrow path breaking off to the left a short way up the facing slope. It is less easy to discern at its outset, but once underfoot this clever contouring path is ideal for incorporating aloof Grey Friar across to the left. It makes a determined bee-line for a similar grassy saddle known as Fairfield, to the right of Grey Friar's bulk, and at a path junction in the saddle a wider path tackles the short pull up to the left onto Grey Friar's outcrop-strewn top. In addition to the main cairn, a prominent lower one to the north begs a visit for its famous prospect of the Scafells.

Swirl How

Steps must be retraced from Grey Friar onto Fairfield, where neither path at the fork is of any use. Instead, Great Carrs, left-hand and least impressive of the two peaks across the col, turns its back to offer a grassy climb up to its top. Gaining the summit is an inspiring moment, for the cairn is found to hover directly above a dramatic plunge to the head of the Greenburn valley. A mere stroll around the rim to the right leads, at last, to the patiently waiting summit of Swirl How, which occupies a near identical position. A little off the path, on the gentle slope to the right just after leaving Great Carrs, may be seen a mute memorial, the remains of an aircraft.

Wetherlam

An almighty cairn towers above the Greenburn face of Swirl How, and within yards of it to the east, a splendid descent of the east ridge commences by way of Prison Band. Though nothing more than an occasional rock step is encountered, a heady mountain atmosphere pervades. Ahead is Wetherlam, the day's final peak, and from the neat col of Swirl Hause the path wastes no time in setting a course for its summit. Such is the urgency that instead of taking the highest ground, in the usual manner, it remains on the Greenburn side of the fell almost all the way, bypassing the subsidiary top of Black Sails up to the right.

Wetherlam's summit cairn stands atop a bouldery dome, and is a fine platform for late in the day views over Little Langdale and Tilberthwaite and across to the Langdale Pikes slotting in above the Blea Tarn gap. A return to Coniston calls for a sharp change of direction to head south, a good path forming to enjoy a graded descent of the broad Lad Stones ridge. When the ground steepens the way swings left over easier ground to eventually come down to join the long, level mine road through Coppermines valley. A left turn will bring a swift return to the village, a more satisfactory conclusion being to cross the Miners Bridge as the track steepens, to follow a pleasanter path down.

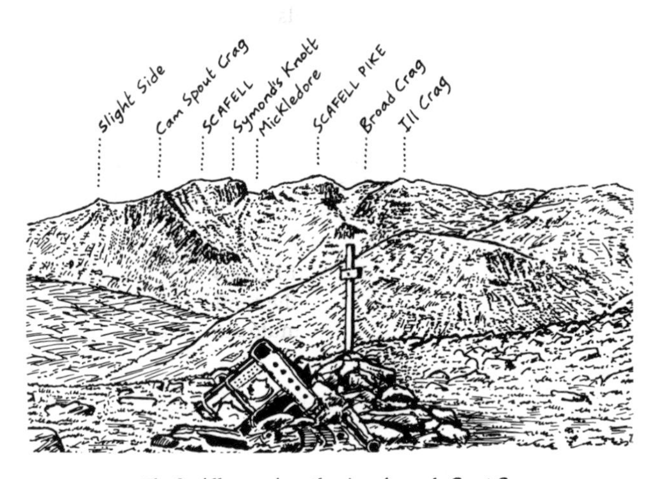

The Scafell range from the aircraft wreck, Great Carrs

WALK 2 PIKE O' BLISCO

L53 **PIKE O' BLISCO** 2312ft/705m

Start: Dungeon Ghyll (285061)
Map: SW Sheet
5 miles / 2200 feet / 2½ - 4 hours
Parking: Dungeon Ghyll Old Hotel

The B5343 Great Langdale road terminates at a minor crossroads just past the hotel drive. Here a narrow road escapes to cross to Little Langdale by way of Blea Tarn, while an unenclosed road begins the walk by heading off through the fields to Stile End. Beyond the farm buildings the Band begins its famous climb to Bowfell, but that path is forsaken for the lower one that remains with the wall on the left. On joining Oxendale Beck a footbridge is soon reached to cross it, and at once the well trodden climb up Pike o' Blisco's northern flank begins. The ravines under Crinkle Crags provide much interest, and the path itself skirts a rough section of Browney Gill. Rising past the cliffs of Black Wars the gradient soon lets up, and a popular crossroads is reached just before the foot of Red Tarn. The left arm resumes the climbing, a clear path covering the last 650 feet up the uniform slope to the summit of Pike o' Blisco.

Cairns of equally impressive dimensions occupy the two highest points, with that to the north stealing the glory on both altitude and merit, particularly as a viewpoint: both the fells and the valley of Langdale are presented in magnificent style. On eventually departing, the path to take is that heading east from the minor depression between the two tops. Beneath a scramble down a small gully an easy, near level section ensues, prior to an eroded descent in the company of Redacre Gill.

In good weather this trying section can be avoided by bearing off to the right before the steep descent starts, and seeking out the higher ground of the extensive eastern shoulder. The cairned top of Long Crag is passed before the better defined Blake Rigg appears farther ahead. Another fine cairn marks its highest point, only yards to the east of which a wall of cliffs brings proceedings to a spectacularly abrupt conclusion.

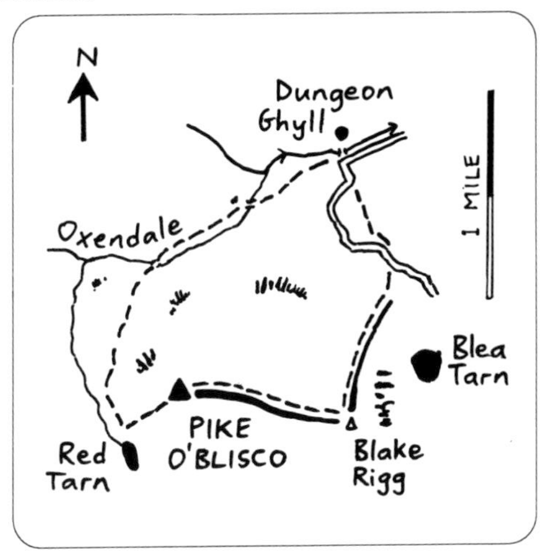

The way off strikes north along the knobbly ridge aiming for the top of the Blea Tarn road. The receding cliffs are kept safely down to the right, with charming views of Blea Tarn backed by Lingmoor Fell. As the road is neared it becomes hidden by an intervening knoll, but on topping it the road summit is just ahead. Directly across is a stile, from where a path turns sharp left to accompany a fence and wall down to a small plantation. From the field below, it enters a campsite, turning left along its drive and onto the road. The hotel is now only minutes away, as is the end of the arresting sight of the Pikes that has held attention throughout the descent.

WALK 3 THE BOWFELL GROUP

L14	**CRINKLE CRAGS**	2818ft/859m
	Shelter Crags	2673ft/815m
L6	**BOWFELL**	2960ft/902m
L10	**ESK PIKE**	2903ft/885m

Start: Brotherilkeld (211011) Map: SW Sheet
13½ miles / 3900 feet / 6½-9½ hours

Parking: at foot of Hardknott Pass (above the cattle-grid above Brotherilkeld) or a little further west along the valley road.

Crinkle Crags

The walk begins along the drive to Brotherilkeld farm, which leaves the road by the phone box at the foot of the pass. The yard need not be entered, as a path heads updale with the river Esk. On release from the constrictions of a fence the path takes a course through pastures to a stile onto the open fell, but soon returns to the river to follow it up to its meeting with Lingcove Beck at Lingcove Bridge. During this beautiful walk, Bowfell's pyramid exerts a magnetic influence ahead.

Not until the end of the walk is the bridge crossed, and for now the route traces a thinner path up the first slopes of the day alongside Lingcove Beck. Higher up, a steady rise leads to a wide loop in the beck, and a divergence of paths at a tiny inflowing marshy beck. By now the flanks of Hard Knott on the right have all but subsided, and a low pass hides the head of Mosedale. Here Lingcove Beck is forsaken for the narrow right fork, heading firmly for the straight line of Swinsty Gill falling from the hollow of Adam-a-Cove on Crinkle Crags' flank. A temptation to take another thin path up to the low pass on the right should be avoided, for beyond a marshy tract the ground

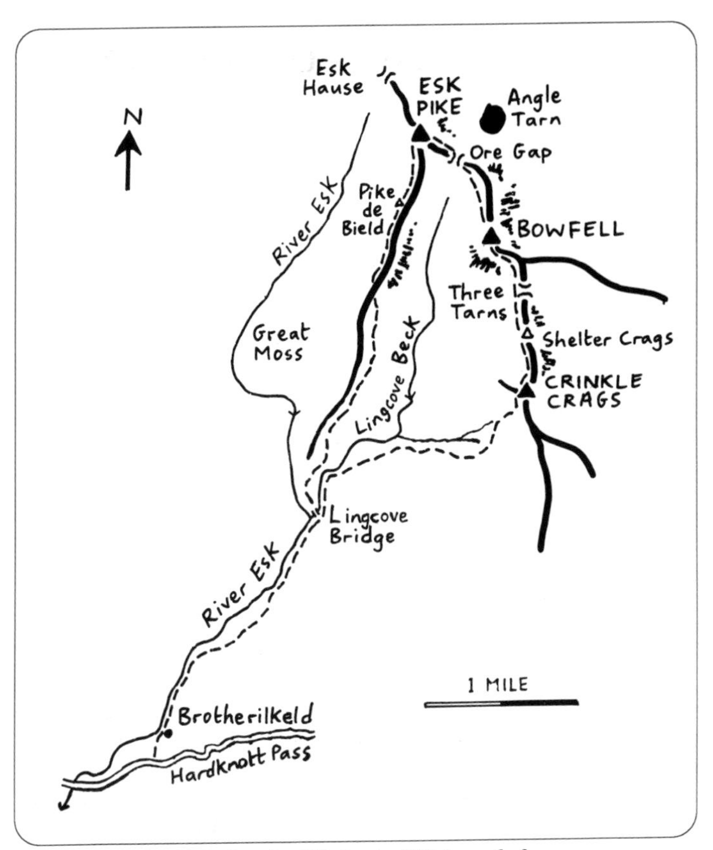

steepens as the right bank of Swinsty Gill is scaled.

Now the ascent begins in earnest, and a slender trod should be located climbing the grassy fellside. In the amphitheatre of Adam-a-Cove the going eases for the remainder of the climb, and the path bears half-left towards the spur of Long Top, highest of the Crinkles. On nearing the summit ridge it fades a little, giving a choice of endings: keeping straight on, the mountain's main ridge is gained at the foot of the Bad Step, and the path taken up through its easy scramble and on to the cairn just beyond. The Bad Step can be omitted by turning left before the main ridge to join a stony, cairned path, the regular flanking route. This gains Long Top just west of the summit cairn.

Bowfell

The traverse to Bowfell is one of Lakeland's great high level walks, on a hugely popular path running north to Three Tarns. Three knobbly Crinkles rise to the north of Long Top, and while the path weaves round them, they scarcely deserve exclusion. Beyond them the path also skirts the slightly lower but greater upthrust of Shelter Crags, whose top is only yards up to the left and also merits a visit. Dropping to the depression of Three Tarns, this is clearly a place to break journey before an assault on the summit of this lofty walk. The climb to Bowfell's cairn is quickly accomplished, but the tiresome nature of the scorched path takes away some of the pleasure. Discerning walkers will, in good conditions, opt for their own variation some way either side of the path. Whatever the route, the bouldery upper reaches of the mountain will soon be underfoot, and two cairned paths set forth from the top of the main climb to gain the summit from either east or south.

Esk Pike

Bowfell's magnificent top is a superb viewpoint, though the summit of unassuming Esk Pike is not particularly prominent. A much trodden and amply cairned path sets off just west of north on a direct course for Ore Gap, the high pass linking the mountains. On a good day this path can be scotched in favour of another that runs north to the top of Hanging Knotts before the short drop to Ore Gap, and affords revealing glimpses of Bowfell's craggy east and north faces as well as a more satisfactory picture of Langdale and the inimitable Pikes. Ore Gap is unmistakable by virtue of the dash of red earth on its very crest, and across it a wide path begins the short and undemanding climb to Esk Pike's summit. The top is marked by a cairn sat just to the north of a large tor-like outcrop.

Descent from Esk Pike is a prolonged affair, involving a full length traverse of its extended south ridge. It is generally broad and grassy but holds some craggy ramparts, and if unfavourable conditions have developed then a better solution is to return to Ore Gap, there turning right on a cairned trod departing from the small cairn on the very summit. It descends in the company of Yeastyrigg Gill, which soon becomes Lingcove Beck alongside which the outward leg is gained on a path fuelled by the addition of a path coming down from Three Tarns.

Esk Pike's south ridge offers unrivalled views of the mountain scenery of upper Eskdale, with Bowfell and the Crinkles on one side and on the other the spectacular line-up of the Scafells, with the subsidiary top of Ill Crag upstaging its illustrious colleagues. It is difficult to detect even the thinnest trod during the initial descent of the ridge, whose first prominent feature is the rocky knoll of Pike de Bield. Two individual cairns sit above the Eskdale flank, and just past them a narrow green way can be picked up at a tiny tarn. This trod bypasses Yeastyrigg Crags just behind the tarn, and comes down through softening terrain to cross to the Lingcove side of the ridge.

After a lengthy spell on the ridge-side the trod drops left towards Lingcove Beck, and is best vacated in favour of keeping to the ridge and Pianet Knott. Dropping right before this prominent tor, a clearer path unfolds as the bracken level is reached, and the green path crosses an old wall to continue down, meeting Lingcove Beck in spectacular mood before ending down the final spur above the confluence. The path coming down from Great Moss is joined for the final few yards back to Lingcove Bridge. A retracing of steps to Brotherilkeld cannot fail to be enjoyed: one is rarely in such hallowed country.

WALK 4 HARTER FELL

L65 **HARTER FELL** 2142ft/653m

Start: Brotherilkeld (211011) Map: SW Sheet
5½ miles / 1900 feet / 3-4 hours
Parking: at foot of Hardknott Pass, above the cattle-grid above Brotherilkeld.

The walk leaves the parking area above the cattle-grid at the foot of the pass without even having to set foot on the road, by taking an inviting little bridge over the adjacent Hardknott Gill West. A good path heads off to the right, steadily at first and then rising more earnestly across the colourful lower slopes of Harter Fell. Though this splendid path barely calls for rest stops, they are certainly required to embrace the rapidly unfolding panorama of Eskdale, from the green valley floor to the mountainous dalehead. Beyond the charming Dodknott Gill it continues up to approach and then climb parallel with the larger Spothow Gill, though never actually crossing it.

Soon the path turns up to the left to commence the rather longer second section of the ascent. Strengthened by merging with the popular path climbing from lower down the valley, the well trodden route forges ever upwards to gain one of Lakeland's grandest summits. The highest point is a splendid rocky tor overlooking a humbled Ordnance column.

In unfavourable conditions, the best return route is to reverse the route of ascent, but in clear weather an interesting and varied return can be made by a prolonged descent incorporating Hardknott Pass. This involves first heading east from the summit to escape the rim of the cliffs, then striking north-east on the broad and in places marshy ridge that eventually leads to the summit of the pass. A thin path can be followed for most of the way, passing near the cliff of Demming Crag

- unseen from above, therefore care needed - and keeping above the deathly darkness of the afforested Duddon flank of the fell.

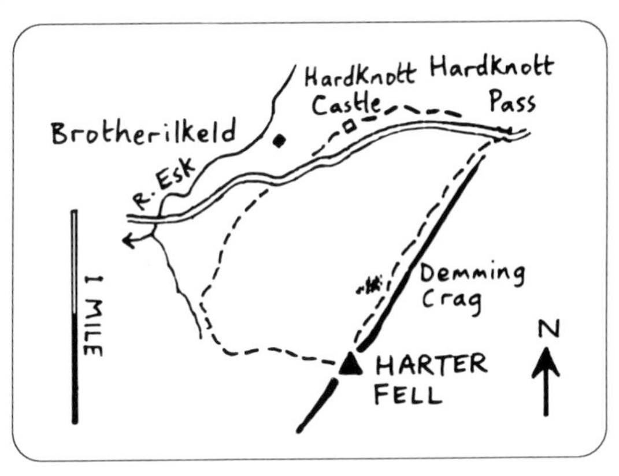

Turning left on gaining the pass, the motor road can be vacated at the first sharp bend beneath the craggy ramparts of Border End, and trods in the bracken traced down to the dramatically sited Hardknott Castle. This Roman fort sits on a ledge high above the floor of Eskdale, and from its far side a green path continues down to a wall corner and concludes on the wide verges of the lower zig-zags of the pass above Brotherilkeld.

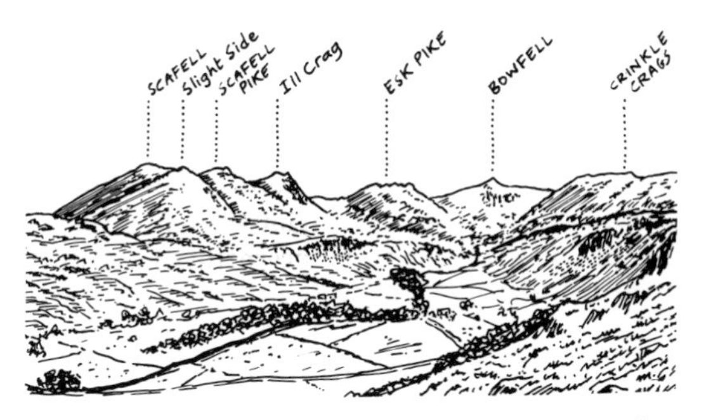

The mountains of upper Eskdale from the slopes of Harter Fell

WALK 5 THE MOUNTAINS OF COPELAND FOREST

L68	**IRON CRAG**	2099+ft/640+m
	Caw Fell	2263+ft/690+m
L29	**HAYCOCK**	2614ft/797m
L56	**SEATALLAN**	2270ft/692m

Start: Nether Wasdale (Harrow Head)
GR 126055 Map: SW & NW Sheets
12 miles / 3600 feet / 6-8½ hours
Parking: Harrow Head is located 1½ miles along the Gosforth road from the junction alongside Wastwater, and there are several off-road verges where the open fell meets the road.

Iron Crag

To the east of Harrow Head a bridleway leaves the road along the drive to Windsor Farm. On levelling out to approach the farm, the bridleway forsakes it to rise steadily to the right. After a brief spell by a wall, the way, not totally distinct here, climbs leisurely to the right through a marshy area. A drove road for bringing sheep off the fell, it soon improves as it breasts the lower slopes of Seatallan to enter the haunting loneliness of upper Blengdale. A slight descent is needed to enter the valley proper, from where the track persists for a good mile and a half until confronted by the valley head.

At the head of Blengdale the track finally expires, and only then is it necessary to turn left with the headwaters of the river to trace its main feeder, Tongue Gill, up the steep flanks of Caw Fell immediately to the left. Keeping to the right of a prominent rash of boulders, the grassy ridge top is gained and crossed to meet a wall that reassuringly traverses it. A right-angle that sees it off along the Ennerdale

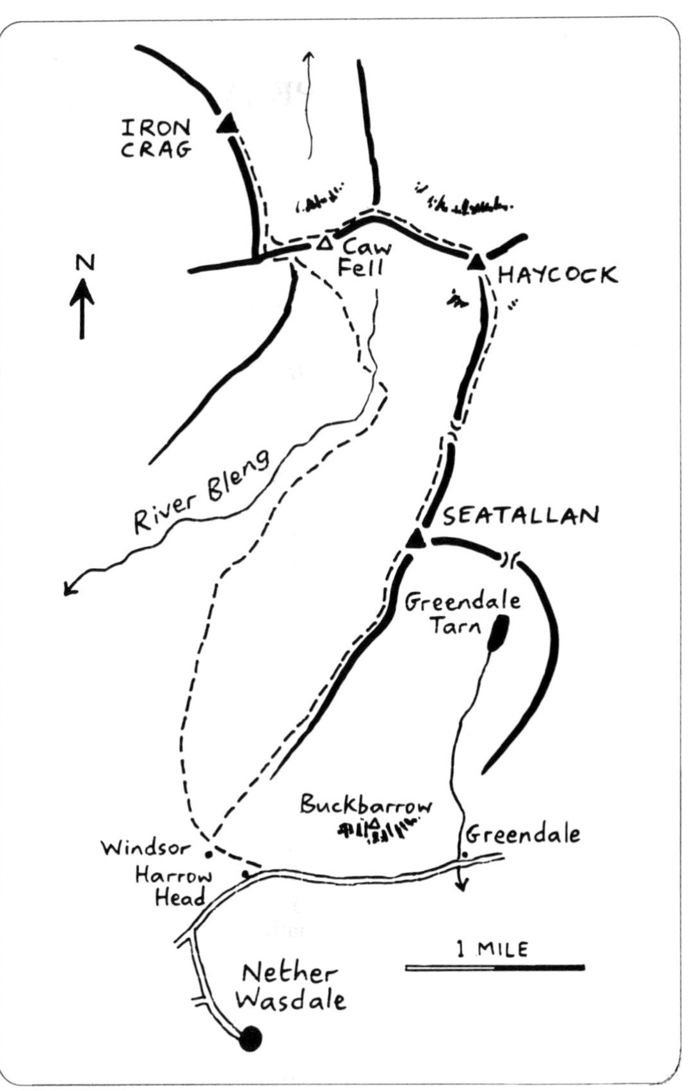
IRON CRAG
N
Caw Fell
HAYCOCK
River Bleng
SEATALLAN
Greendale Tarn
Buckbarrow
Greendale
Windsor
Harrow Head
1 MILE
Nether Wasdale

watershed should be located ahead or a little to the left: it is the key to Iron Crag, which can be seen less than a mile to the north. A path shadows the wall down to the saddle and up onto Iron Crag's broad top, and the cairn, only yards from the wall, is gained by crossing it at any suitable gap during the climb.

Haycock

From Iron Crag the skyline walk to Haycock is laid out, first task being to return to Caw Fell's plateau. A thin path leaves the wall during the re-ascent to cut out its angle, and once on top it is a short stroll to the summit cairn near the wall on Caw Fell. After the barest of descents a longer but undemanding climb leads to Haycock's stony top. Two features along the way are the wall itself, which keeps an eye on the slim path, and the rough tor of Little Gowder Crag.

Seatallan

From Haycock, rounded Seatallan is firmly in view to the south, though a bee-line is not practicable. Unseen is a rough flank bearing Gowder Crag, so the first step is to cross to the prominent south cairn. Here routes either south-east or south-west can be chosen to reach the wide saddle before Seatallan, and while both encounter moderately rough terrain, neither presents difficulties. Below the rougher ground rapid progress is made into the depression, and though marshy in parts a green trod can be picked up to gain Seatallan's drier contours. The path fades on the steeper ground, but natural grassy steps assist in nearing the bleak top, where a small cairn points the way to a sprawling tumulus of a cairn and an Ordnance column.

A pathless and generally uneventful descent begins by heading south-west down the ever broadening flank, and a direct route maintaining this course will meet the drove road above Windsor. In good weather a rewarding finish can be enjoyed by veering south as the ridge expands further, to a prominent cairn on Glade How. Below it, another cairn stands atop the cliffs of Buckbarrow, offering superb views across Wastwater to the Screes and the Scafell group. Care is needed in the final descent, the answer being to go right, well above the crags, to locate a path that drops pleasantly down in the company of Gill Beck. It joins the road 400 yards east of the start.

WALK 6 THE MOSEDALE ROUND

L70	**YEWBARROW**	2060ft/628m
	Stirrup Crag	2020ft/616m
	Red Pike	2709ft/826m
L20	**SCOAT FELL**	2758ft/841m
	Steeple	2686ft/819m
	Black Crag	2716ft/828m
L8	**PILLAR**	2927ft/892m
	Looking Stead	2057ft/627m

Start: Wastwater (Overbeck Bridge)
GR 168068 Map: SW Sheet
12 miles / 4200 feet / 6-9 hours
Parking: roadside car park

Yewbarrow

From the car park a path runs by Over Beck to a gate to begin what looks an unremitting climb up the ridge of Yewbarrow. A pleasant green path proves far less demanding than anticipated, soon reaching a stile from where the path escapes to the left in the face of a craggy bluff. Climbing soon restarts up a stony shoot that narrows to squeeze between crags, scrambling opportunities arising before an easier pull up to a memorable arrival at the Great Door, with Wastwater and the Scafells looming across this brief knife edge section of the ridge. Before the climb to the Great Door, a well trodden path breaks off left to omit this classic moment, gaining the ridge at a similar, less inspiring notch. Several minor outcrops interrupt what now becomes a grassy and increasingly gentle stroll up to the summit cairn, located a long way back from the action.

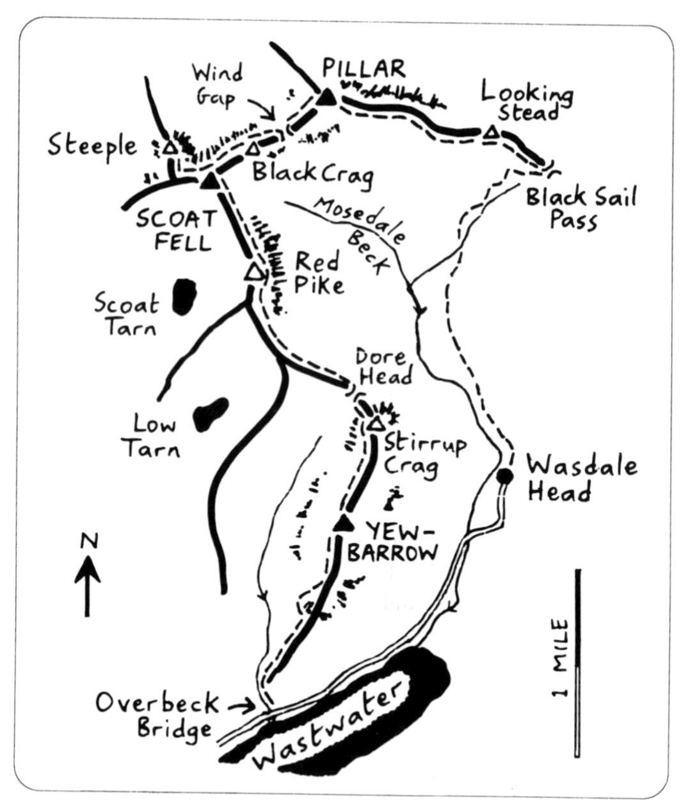

The path continues north along the broad ridge, crossing a depression before a short pull to the cairn on Stirrup Crag. The descent from here is fascinating, first twisting down to another cairn as eyes are fixed on the grassy saddle of Dore Head, several hundred feet below. Apprehension mounts as the top of the crag is reached, from where eyes are better fixed on the task in hand. It comes as a surprise to find that excepting icy conditions, this scrambly descent is not fraught with difficulties. A well worn route - the only way - spirals down a clever series of chimneys and clefts between bands of rock, hands not being the only parts of the anatomy to be pressed into service. All too soon the escapade is over, and the path zig-zags down through scree to the sanctuary of Dore Head.

Scoat Fell

The climb to Red Pike, one of the finest of subsidiary tops, is almost a full ascent in its own right: the gentle nature of the walk belies the amount of climbing involved. What is possibly the least worn of Lakeland's major ridge paths makes its way effortlessly up the facing slope, forking below a rash of boulders near the top. While the path to the right is a little easier, the one climbing through the rocks holds more interest, and at the top has the bonus of visiting The Chair, a rock platform fashioned into a seat with the addition of some of the many stones scattered around. Only a hundred yards beyond is the prominent south top, after which a simple stroll leads to the summit cairn, perched atop a dark abyss above Mosedale. For some reason a distinct path from the south top gives the summit a wide berth, opting to contour round to the left.

Next on the ridge, Scoat Fell offers its least interesting flank. From Red Pike's summit the path adheres to the Mosedale edge, soon falling to a high saddle before re-climbing. Almost at once the path of those in a hurry swings right to cut Scoat Fell out of the deal: when its intentions become clear, a string of cairns encourage an obvious departure up the grassy slope in front. A rash of small boulders is crossed before arrival at the wall that traverses the summit. The main cairn is to be found on the other side of one of the gaps, although some bright spark has erected a smaller version on the wall top.

Pillar

While the walk turns north-east with the wall, those with ample energy will grasp the opportunity to detour onto the airy top of Steeple, which thrusts itself so vehemently into the scene across Mirk Cove. It is probably fairly safe to permit the luxury of leaving a rucksack by Scoat Fell's cairn to enjoy the novelty of an unburdened 20 minutes. The job in hand, however, cannot be long delayed, for hoary Pillar is all too evident beyond the top of Black Crag. The wall cuts out of the scene abruptly as the descent starts, on a good path whose fall is broken by Black Crag's neat top. From its cairn, stony ground paves the way for a short descent to Wind Gap. To gain a foothold on Pillar a web of interwoven routes awaits, and the initially steep pull is best enjoyed by tackling the rocks directly in front. The going soon relents and the path eases itself onto Pillar's extensive summit plateau, with a shelter in the centre marking the highest point.

Pillar is departed to the south-east, down the prolonged east ridge to Black Sail Pass. A much trodden path keeps generally close to the line of defunct fence posts, and that it takes a mile and a half to lose 1100 feet is evidence of the ease of the task. With a good mile of the ridge underfoot, fence posts rise left to the grassy dome of Looking Stead, which can be easily incorporated if only for a break from the path. The top of Black Sail Pass is marked by a long redundant and rather incongruous iron gate, and, to the Wasdale side, a cairn.

From the path junction, that to the right is needed, passing the cairn to commence the second half of the long descent to Wasdale. The well pounded track drops down into Mosedale to conclude in relaxed fashion, entering Wasdale Head by a short lane alongside the beck to emerge at the side of the hotel. Unfortunately, a little more legwork remains if Overbeck Bridge must be regained, though the long mile and a half along the road is more than compensated, even at this late stage, by the surround of mountains, notably Gable and the Scafells.

Pillar from Wasdale Head

WALK 7 THE SCAFELL GROUP

L28	**LINGMELL**	2624+ft/800+m
L1	**SCAFELL PIKE**	3208ft/978m
L2	**SCAFELL**	3162ft/964m

Start: Wasdale Head Map: SW Sheet
9 miles / 4000 feet / 5½-8 hours
Parking: car park in the hamlet, and on the green before it.

Lingmell

The walk leaves the green by the rough lane past the church to Brackenthwaite, behind which a wide green path bears right for Lingmell Beck. Two hundred yards beyond the bridge over inflowing Gable Beck the path forks: the main arm rises across Great Gable's flank, while a thin trod keeps faith with the beck. This latter option is an easy stroll into the heart of the mountains, with Great End straight ahead and the Great Napes on Gable towering above. Shortly before the confluence with Spouthead Gill from the left, the ultimate goal of Scafell Pike briefly reveals itself, tantalisingly high beyond the turrets above Piers Gill.

On crossing Spouthead Gill at the confluence, the path zig-zags up the grassy tongue in between to a cairn. At this point the main path is again forsaken in favour of a right branch, an initially shy path which keeps well above the bed of the beck to rise to cross the next side-stream of Greta Gill just above its confluence. On the right now the ravine of Piers Gill begins to take shape, and the path keeps well above the edge of this magnificent cleft: minor diversions are needed to peer in, but not to appraise the jagged pinnacles topping Lingmell Crag.

The dog-leg of Piers Gill is turned at a delightful scramble to continue up to meet the Corridor Route from Sty Head just as it crosses the upper ravine. Turning right along it, the main path bound more directly for Scafell Pike is soon left on a slender, cairned trod across a green hollow on the right, over a ruinous wall to gain the Lingmell Col. A short pull up the path to the right will quickly have Lingmell's summit underfoot.

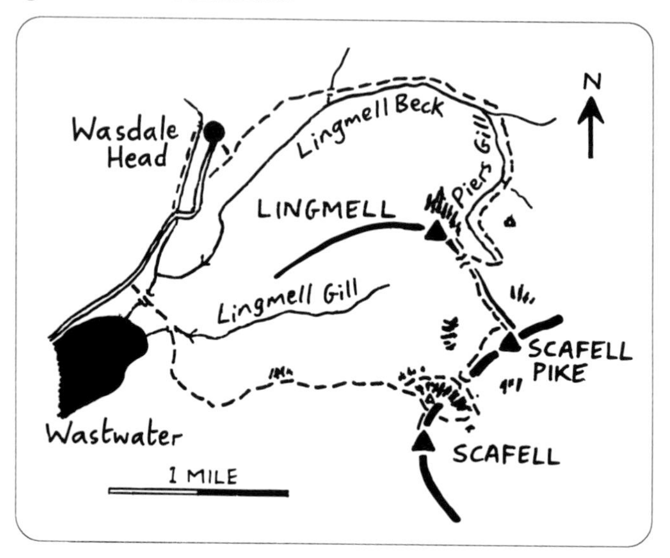

Scafell Pike

From Lingmell's cairn steps are retraced to the col, from where the sprawling upper slopes of the Pike must be faced. Climbing directly up, the path is soon reinforced by the Corridor Route path and the Wasdale 'tourist' route. Together they scale the bouldery uppermost 500 feet of England's highest acres, to gain the mighty platform that rises above all else.

Scafell

From the Pike's summit the obstacles presented by Scafell's awesome face are often in shadow, and unable to be appreciated until neared. The key to the crossing to Scafell is Mickledore, a lofty grass ridge linking the two great peaks, a thrilling place to be but also one to make hearts sink. It is gained by starting back along the route of ascent, but within 200 yards taking the left fork at a profusely cairned junction to descend steadily to the famous saddle. At this end of Mickledore is a stretcher box, and at the far end, the wall of Scafell Crag.

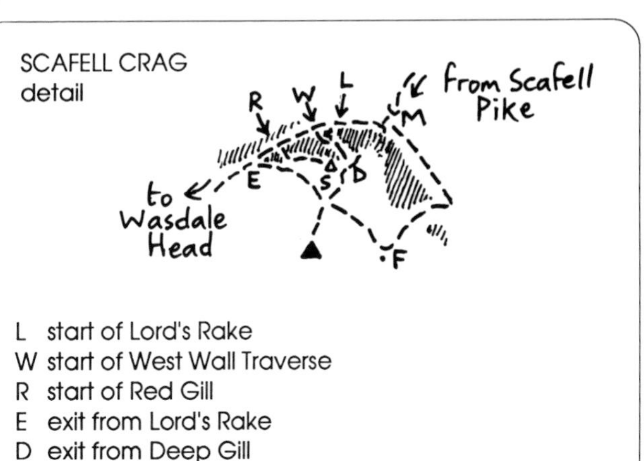

On Mickledore decisions are made: with the face of Scafell Crag emphatically denying a direct route, and infamous Broad Stand a non-starter to the average fellwalker, two options exist. Both demand considerable loss of height, and differ in character if not in roughness. The Foxes Tarn route calls for greater descent but is generally less arduous, turning left to drop down a scree-filled enclave bound for Cam Spout. In about 300 yards a much-used gully signals a break in the defensive crags, and a rough scramble leads up to the tiny pool. In improved conditions the path turns right up to a grassy saddle between unseen Scafell Crag, right, and the summit, sat up to the left.

The second option is the renowned Lord's Rake route, heading down to the right off the far end of Mickledore. An obvious path, a little insecure in places, skirts the base of the crag to reach the unmistakable foot of the great gully that is the start of the Rake. A scramble up this eroded stone shoot is remote from fellwalking, and is an experience unlikely to be forgotten. Wherever possible, the least difficult approach is to make use of the more solid rock at the sides, while at all times being vigilant for the greatest danger, that of a pedestrian above sending a shower of rocks down the gully. The tidiest of cols marks the end of the suffering: two more gentle ups and downs lead to the end of the cliffs and thus the Rake. A stony but simple rise then gains the saddle between the unseen Scafell Crag, left, and the summit, across to the right.

Lingmell and Piers Gill from the Corridor Route

Adventurous souls can prolong the thrills by vacating the Rake at either of two points. The first comes just before arrival on the first col, where a ledge departs left to enter Deep Gill for a rough clamber up to the summit plateau: this is the West Wall Traverse, which passes through rock scenery of total grandeur. Rather less demanding is a sortie up Red Gill, which reveals itself up to the left from the last depression before the end of Lord's Rake: a left fork marks the start of the pull up to it, and once up the gully a climb to the left leads to the top of Symond's Knott, above Deep Gill. Both these exceedingly rough but absorbing routes share the bonus of having to retrace less steps on returning from the summit.

The return to Wasdale Head begins by first making for the exit of Lord's Rake. If not having used the full length of the Rake in ascent, then it is reached by first returning north towards the saddle, a cairned path then dropping half-left to the rim of the crags above the Rake. Now turning directly away from the clifftops, the path soon leaves the bouldery upper slopes and descends an increasingly grassy shoulder, though at Rakehead Crags it opts for skirting their rim in adventurous fashion.

Bearing left down the grass once more, and avoiding a stony rake dropping extremely steeply right after Rakehead Crags, the path soon steepens, straight down the grassy flank to a stile in a fence. The enclosure below leads down to another fence, turning right with it to a stile then down again to meet the track descending from Burnmoor. Turning down it past a climbing hut, it runs out onto the road above the head of Wastwater. The short mile to the hamlet can be broken up by taking a footpath along Mosedale Beck's west bank at Down in the Dale Bridge, ending stylishly over the packhorse bridge behind the hotel.

Lingmell, Scafell Pike and Scafell from Wastwater

WALK 8 THE GABLE GROUP

L26	**KIRK FELL**	2631ft/802m
	-East top	2581ft/787m
L7	**GREAT GABLE**	2949ft/899m
	Green Gable	2627ft/801m
L49	**BRANDRETH**	2345ft/715m

Start: Honister Pass Map: NW Sheet
9½ miles / 3600 feet / 5-7½ hours
Parking: car park by youth hostel on summit of pass.

Kirk Fell

On this walk all the day's tops are passed on the outward leg, before turning to commence a classic high level switchback. From the road outside the hostel a gate leads into a quarry yard, across which a rough road heads off to the right. This is soon vacated by a stony path on the left, which is a variation start to the eroded lower section of the old tramway to Dubs Quarry. Soon easier ground is encountered, and remains the norm all the way to Black Sail Pass. At the highest point of the tramway is the site of the Drum House, which held its winding gear: here a cairned path branches left, commencing a lengthy section of the centuries-old trading route of Moses' Trod.

The trod is now a modern walkers' highway as far as Beck Head between Great Gable and Kirk Fell, but there remain a couple of points where caution is needed to avoid a wrong turn. Rising gently across the western flanks of Grey Knotts, the first junction, amply cairned, sees a path to Black Sail Hut at the head of Ennerdale contour off to the right. A little further, on Brandreth's flanks, the main path rises left to Gillercomb Head, bound for Great Gable: here, crossing the line of the old boundary fence, it is necessary to keep straight on, dropping slightly to retrieve the old course of the trod. Full length views of the Buttermere valley give way to views down Ennerdale as Green Gable's flank leads to Stone Cove under Windy Gap, and a steady rise well below the towering cliffs of Gable itself. A short descent then leads to the important col of Beck Head.

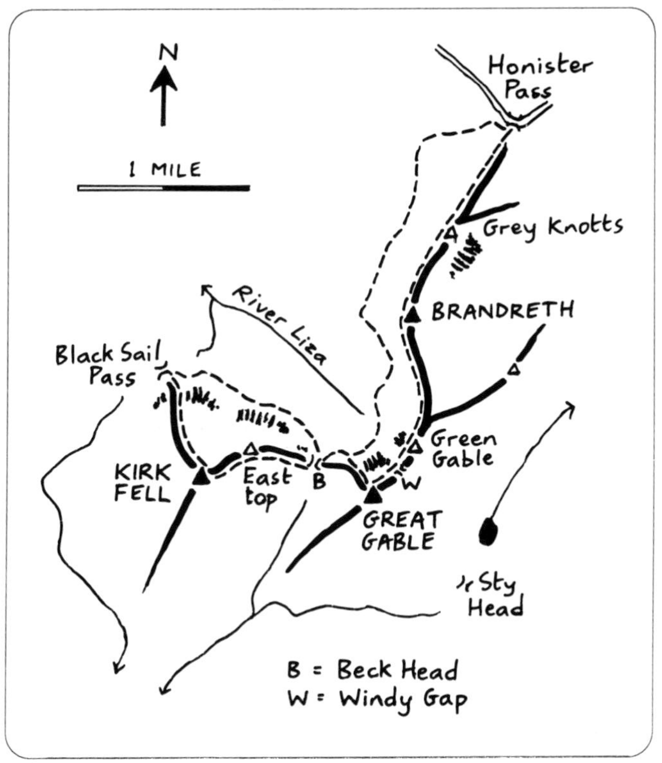

Across Beck Head stands the bulk of Kirk Fell, and an obvious direct ascent can be effected by taking the stony path up Rib End. Far more rewarding, however, is the roundabout approach 'from the back,' which gives a better climb as well as saving a retracing of steps. At the far end of the col a path can be seen cutting down to the right: its aim is to traverse the northern flank of the mountain to Black Sail Pass, while losing as little height as possible. This it does most successfully, with towering cliffs above and Ennerdale far below, and only a mild re-ascent needed to gain the top of Black Sail Pass.

On Black Sail Pass the decidedly more demanding return begins by turning up to the left. Crags of all shapes and sizes line this north-western shoulder of Kirk Fell, but a most enjoyable pull, keeping close to the line of old fenceposts, ensures an absorbing ascent with the occasional mini-scramble presenting itself. When the going relents, the defunct fenceposts serve to point the way over the extensive top to the summit cairn.

Great Gable

To the east Great Gable appears a formidable and curiously-shaped object, and to set foot on it the broad top is crossed, the path actually outflanking the East top to its south. A descent of Rib End then follows to return to the familiar environs of Beck Head. After a short climb to regain Moses' Trod, the ascent begins in earnest, continuing directly up Gable's bouldery north-western shoulder on a zig-zagging path that is less of a trial than it might appear. At the top a few easier strides lead to one of Lakeland's favourite summits.

Brandreth

The ridgewalk to Brandreth passes over intervening Green Gable, though neither top is visible from Great Gable's summit. They soon appear, however, as a well trodden path sets off north, soon swinging east, across the boulder-strewn felltop. The unseen precipice of Gable Crag deflects the path - a boot-worn ribbon upon the thousands of rocks - around its eastern edge to a rough descent onto the slim defile of Windy Gap. The dusty red path opposite offers a short pull onto the top of Green Gable, from where Gable Crag can now be satisfactorily appraised from a position of security.

A well blazed path sets off down Green Gable's northern slopes, many of its users being ushered right at a well cairned fork to Seathwaite by way of Gillercomb. Beyond the three tarns in the cradle of Gillercomb Head, the path swings left to rise across Brandreth's flank for a slightly easier return to Honister. As it becomes clear that it will not lead to Brandreth's summit, the faithful Ennerdale fence-posts should be joined in a climb up the broken slope to the right. A thin, discreetly cairned path takes only two minutes to gain Brandreth's flat top.

North-east of Brandreth the broad ridge marches relentlessly on across a minor depression to Grey Knotts, where tarns and tors add character to the final top of the day. The way off is north-east, a thin path descending through low outcrops to meet a fence that drops down to Honister Pass. The path crosses at a stile near the top, then shadows it all the way down, steeply in parts, to the pass, in sight long before it is reached.

The Gables from Black Sail Hut, Ennerdale

WALK 9 THE SEATHWAITE ROUND

L5	**GREAT END**	2984ft/910m
	Allen Crags	2575ft/785m
	Lincomb Tarns Top	2365ft/721m
	Looking Steads	2542ft/775m
L32	**GLARAMARA**	2568ft/783m

Start: Seathwaite
GR 235121 Map: NW & SW Sheets
8 miles / 3350 feet / 4½-6½ hours
Parking: at the end of the road at Seathwaite farm.

Great End

Seathwaite is departed through the farmyard and out on a broad track to soon make closer acquaintance with the river Derwent. Beyond the meeting of Styhead Gill and Grains Gill to form the Derwent, the latter is crossed at Stockley Bridge and a hugely popular path begins its climb. The going eases as the path parallels Styhead Gill, crossing it at a simple footbridge and soon gaining Styhead Tarn: just beyond it are the boulder and stretcher box on the summit of Sty Head Pass. Alternatively the tarn can be reached by turning right through Seathwaite's farm buildings to a footbridge over the river, then turning left on a path that soon climbs, steeply alongside Taylorgill Force, to meet the other path at the bridge before the tarn.

At Sty Head a left turn (eastwards) takes the broad path bound for Esk Hause. Directly ahead is the bony rib of the Band tumbling from the summit plateau of Great End, and this spur provides a natural and rewarding stairway to the top. Whilst a thin path breaks off the Esk Hause path just before crossing the parallel beck, the purist's route involves tackling the Band immediately, and outflanking several small outcrops before a tiny saddle signals the arrival of the aforementioned path.

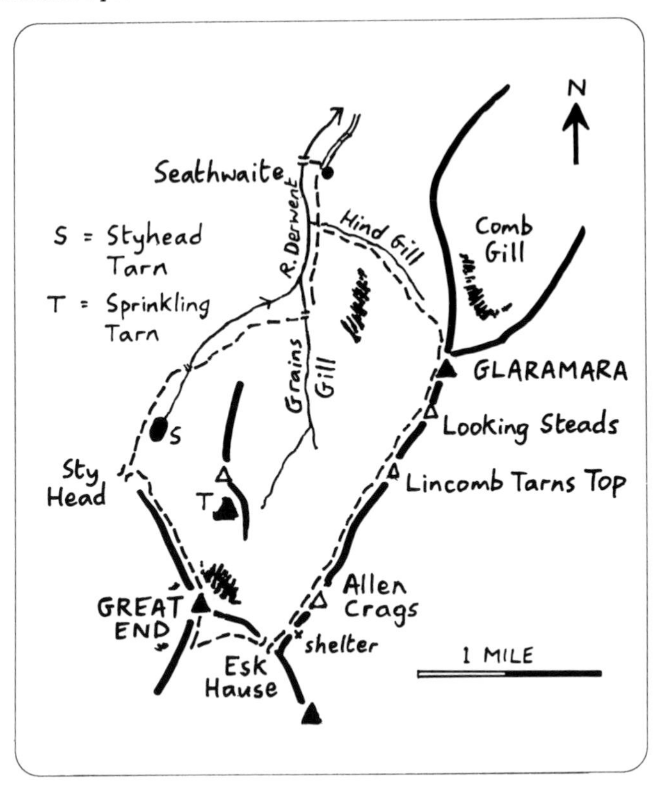

The path takes a fairly clear line up the Band, pausing for respite at a neat little trough marking the start of the great ravine of Skew Gill, not apparent as such here. Above this the going roughens a little, with the occasional simple scramble leading up through minor crags. Boulders increase in both size and presence as the top is neared, and the final spell of work heralds arrival on easier ground above the cleft of Custs Gully. Set a little further back is the north-west cairn with adjacent shelter, viewpoint for Wasdale and Gable, while across a grassy depression is the marginally higher summit cairn.

In all but bad conditions the Band holds no terrors, but if need be an easier option continues up Grains Gill from Stockley Bridge, intersecting the Esk Hause path and following it up to the shelter under the pass. The well blazed Scafell Pike path then slants up to the col above Calf Cove, from where a path breaks off across easy ground to rise up to Great End's top.

Glaramara

The next objective from Great End is the intervening top of Allen Crags, and Esk Hause is the key to it. Although a rough path heads south-east from Great End's cairn, easier going can be found by heading south to the Calf Cove col, thence joining the Scafell Pike brigade to descend to the true Esk Hause, 100 feet above the famous shelter. At this point the energetic can choose to incorporate Esk Pike into the outing, an extra half hour, at least, being required for the climb up the slope opposite and subsequent return to the pass. If this does not appeal (or the better excuse of saving it for Walk 3 is used), then a descent towards the wall shelter should be made. Passing straight by it the path up to Allen Crags cannot be mistaken, and its twin summit cairns will be alongside within minutes.

From Allen Crags the bulk of Glaramara lies in wait along the ridge, and a clear path links the two in splendid fashion. Intervening ups and downs occur with regularity, the main saddle at High House and Lincomb Tarns being followed by rises over Lincomb Tarns Top and within yards of the top of Looking Steads, also referred to as Glaramara's third summit. When the main summit is gained it is almost with disbelief, and even then possibly only after breasting the south-west top which is probably of equal altitude. It hides the main top and hovers only yards from and above the path doggedly seeking its goal. When it is reached, however, it cannot be mistaken, though in mist there is ample scope for confusion.

The rocky summit tower stands above a craggy drop to the north, and the easiest path off returns south-west to the depression between the two tops before turning north. An alternative heads north-east, and almost at once encounters a rock barrier that brings hands and probably rear quarters into use, and though the scramble is straightforward, it may perhaps be a little off-putting from above for the unwary. The ridge running north from the summit is the traditional route of descent, a good path running along the crest of Thornythwaite Fell and directly down to Borrowdale. Both paths departing the summit have this as their target, but the easier western option is also a sure pointer to the lesser known descent to Seathwaite.

The left-hand path off the top is, despite being profusely cairned, only a thin green trod as it descends steadily to the western rim of the felltop. Here the cairns tempt one across the embryo Hind Gill and attendant marshy tract and continue along the ridge, when in fact the required route turns left before the beck, and with no more cairns nor even a thin trod, hesitantly sets off over the grassy edge. Remaining close to the beck a thin trod soon resurrects itself, as do the cairns a little farther down, each being tidily perched on a boulder.

As the white-walled buildings of Seathwaite come into view far below, the slope steepens, the cairns increase, and the path suddenly becomes very clear. This steep section does not last unduly long, and lower down it has the reward of smashing glimpses into a now substantial ravine bedecked with colourful vegetation. At a gate in the intake wall the gradient eases, and though the path loses itself by the beck it matters not as the valley bottom is just ahead. At the bottom of the pasture the beck is crossed to a gate giving access to the track on which the walk commenced, just short of Seathwaite.

WALK 10 THE CENTRAL RIDGE

	Pike o'Stickle	2326ft/709m
	Loft Crag	2230+ft/680+m
L44	**HARRISON STICKLE**	2414ft/736m
	Thunacar Knott	2371ft/723m
L40	**HIGH RAISE**	2499ft/762m
L48	**ULLSCARF**	2381ft/726m
	Low Saddle	2152ft/656m

Start: Stonethwaite Map: SW & NW Sheets
13½ miles / 3400 feet / 6-9 hours
Parking: limited in the hamlet itself, but a broad verge on the road on the way in offers more room.

Harrison Stickle

Sequestered Stonethwaite provides a delightful start and finish to a walk that offers a rare approach to the Langdale Pikes - from 'behind.' The way departs where signposted for the Stake Pass, passing the hotel and dividing into a choice of field path or walled lane. Reuniting near the confluence of Greenup Gill and Langstrath Beck, the route continues up the bank of the latter. A little farther, with the valley stretching ahead and living up to its name, the beck is crossed at a footbridge, though paths follow either bank to another bridge two miles on.

Midway, the gorge at Blackmoss Pot calls for inspection, and on passing the second footbridge the point of departure from the valley is reached. While Langstrath continues on, a tiny bridge over inflowing Stake Beck is the signal to take a path ascending its right bank:

a series of exquisite zig-zags will be lapped up by the discerning walker. When the climb ends a short stroll leads to the tarn and cairn on the summit of Stake Pass.

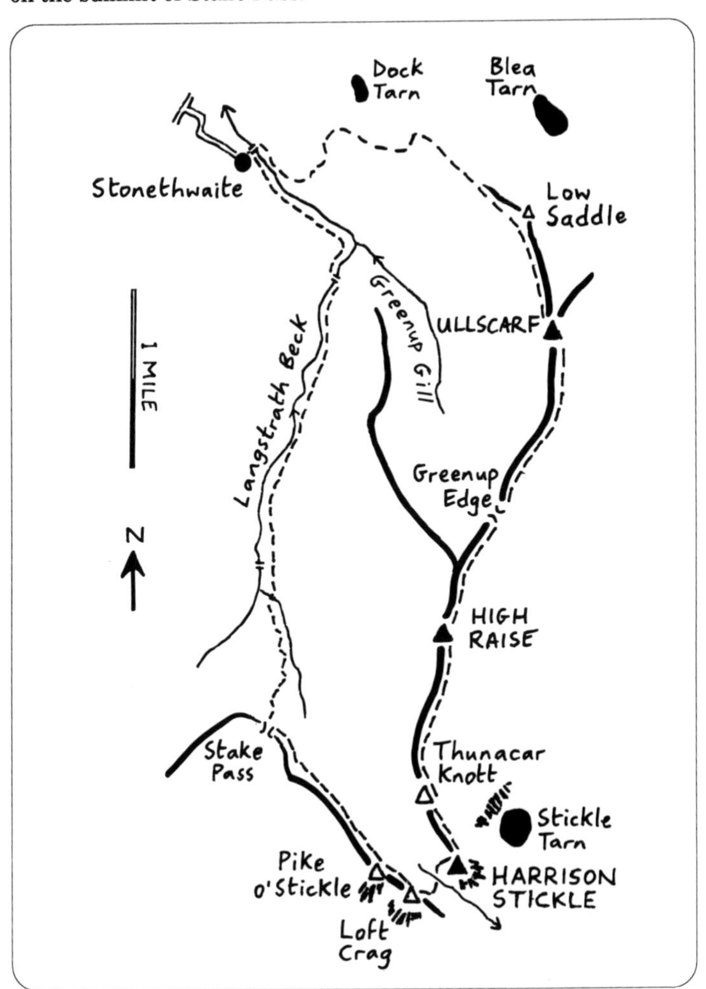

At the cairn a clear path heads off to the left, aiming for the prominent peak of Pike o'Stickle, the only Langdale Pike as yet visible. Reinforced almost at once by a path from the Langdale side of the pass, the way rises across Martcrag Moor, with its very soft centre. When Pike o'Stickle re-appears for good, one is virtually at the foot of its summit cone. A path sneaks left to circumvent the ascent, but there is little justification for omitting this classic top: a mild scramble adds to the all too brief pleasure in gaining the limited space up above.

From Pike o'Stickle, flat-topped Harrison Stickle looms large across the marshy hollow of Harrison Combe. Only ten minutes to the east, however, is Pike o'Stickle's natural twin, Loft Crag: though a path below the tor of Pike o'Stickle heads directly for Harrison Stickle, the well trodden one round the head of the scree shoot to Loft Crag holds more appeal. Having gained this second top of the day, sights can firmly be set on the highest of the Langdale Pikes. Continuing east a short distance from Loft Crag's cairn, a path branching down to the left should be taken to secure a relatively dry crossing of Dungeon Ghyll before it leaves the combe. Rising up the opposite side the path from Dungeon Ghyll is joined and an all too obvious path scales the 300 feet up to the summit of Harrison Stickle.

High Raise

Having consumed the delights of the Langdale scene, eyes and steps must turn north, where the rounded top of Thunacar Knott sits to the left of its similarly shaped parent, High Raise, behind. Turning west from the highest cairn the main path drops down to the north, narrowing as walkers have branched off right for Pavey Ark or Stickle Tarn. A brief rise leads up to the cairn on Thunacar Knott, and continues straight past it with sights firmly targeted on High Raise. As the longer but still effortless plod to High Raise commences, two paths branch off to the peak of Sergeant Man, but the main highway keeps on to soon reach the Ordnance column and shelter on the summit.

Ullscarf

Ullscarf is the last 2000 foot mountain on the ridge, and the route thereto is plainly obvious. The path first heads north-east to a prominent cairn on an outcrop, then traces the main watershed with its occasional fenceposts. Running north to another tor on Low White Stones, the path quickly falls to the saddle of Greenup, a much used pass linking Borrowdale with Grasmere. From its cairned top the path becomes sketchier, and the wider Borrowdale path, which heads off to the left, should not be mistaken for it. Much marshy ground and more surviving fenceposts are encountered north of the pass, relief coming as the drier final contours are reached. Even so, the concluding pull will seem prolonged at this late stage of the walk.

From Ullscarf's summit cairn the descent begins by going north along the watershed. At an angle of an intact fence the route turns left with it, a choice of stiles easing its crossing in order to continue down the broad ridge when the fence darts off to the left. The upthrust of High Saddle is gained just beyond the fence, from where a thin green trod can be followed down to the prominent alp of Low Saddle. The path evades the pull onto it by skirting round to the left, and by this stage few are likely to make the detour. As a steeper drop through a few boulders begins, the path all but fizzles out, though the chosen direction remains the same, north-west to the waiting marshy plateau on this side of Great Crag's heathery knolls.

While crossing the depression a conspicuous wall to the left is seen, acting as boundary between this wild upland and the steep fellside below. Once across, it can be picked up and followed right, possibly over one or two minor undulations depending on the point it was joined. Past the prominent tower of High Crag, almost traversed by the wall, a far more pronounced dip with its own stream is found, and up the opposite bank a cairn marks arrival on the path up to Dock Tarn from the valley.

Turning down the path, the wall is breached at a stile, and the descent to the Stonethwaite valley commences. After initial meandering the path soon drops steeply through an oak wood on a remarkable series of restored zig-zags. This has transformed into a splendid route that steepness and erosion would otherwise have made tortuous. The Greenup path is joined on the valley floor, and just along to the right Stonethwaite Bridge leads back into the hamlet.

WALK 11 FLEETWITH PIKE

L67 **FLEETWITH PIKE** 2125ft/648m

Start: Gatesgarth (194149) Map: NW Sheet
4 miles / 1800 feet / 2-3 hours
Parking: roadside car park opposite farm

From the car park a short stroll along the road leads to the open fell below Fleetwith Pike. Ignoring the broad path heading right, the Fleetwith path soon materialises to commence an immediate assault on the very foot of the ridge, directly ahead. The climb's popularity has resulted in a restored zig-zag section up past the century-old white memorial cross before slanting up onto the crest of the ridge. A grassy interlude is soon eclipsed as Fleetwith Edge takes shape in the heather. The retrospective views of the Buttermere valley call for regular halts, and the final 500 feet in particular form a delectable staircase to the summit, reached all too soon if this fell is the sole objective of a walk.

An interesting return can be effected whilst conducting a little exploration of Fleetwith's hinterland. From the cairn a path heads east, lesser branches adventurously skirting the tops of the mighty cliffs of Honister Crag, to arrive at a pool below the dramatically sited cairned peak of Black Star, hovering above the crags. At this point the path abandons the edge and turns south-east, descending pleasantly to pass quarry remains on the right, crossing over a quarry road and the old road from Honister Pass to Dubs Quarry. During this steady descent the course of the old tramway - again linking Honister and Dubs - will be located below, and its highest point, the remains of the Drum House, backed by Grey Knotts, is the objective. Now utilised as a popular pathway, it can be followed down to the right to the substantial remains at Dubs, entering the site in style through a

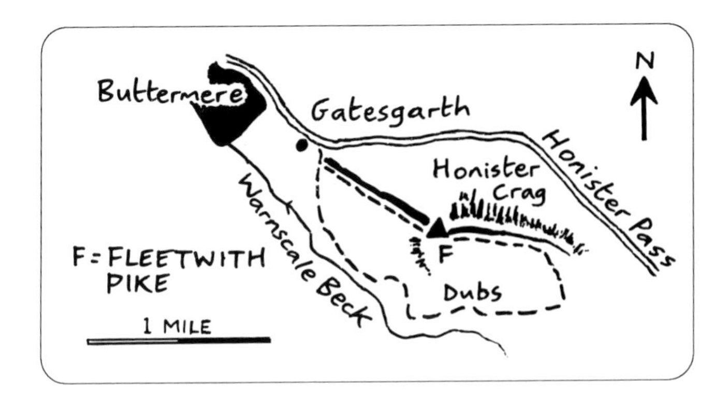

cutting in slate walls.

The path continues beyond the workings, ignoring a branch left which drops down to cross the beck in Dubs Bottom, and soon loses height more rapidly as it runs above a ravine occupied by Warnscale Beck. On swinging away from the beck, this excellent, broad path, which also once served the quarry, inevitably, curves down the lower flanks of Fleetwith Pike into Warnscale Bottom, quickly returning to the road where the walk began.

Fleetwith Pike from Buttermere

WALK 12 THE BUTTERMERE FELLS

L23	**HIGH STILE**	2647ft/807m
	Red Pike	2476ft/755m
L69	**STARLING DODD**	2076ft/633m
L71	**GREAT BORNE**	2020ft/616m

Start: Buttermere Map: NW Sheet
11 miles / 3300 feet / 5½-8 hours
Parking: large car park in village.

High Stile

From Buttermere a wealth of delightful paths radiate, and the most popular is the fenced track that runs to the left of the Fish Hotel to the foot of the lake. After crossing both the outflow and Sour Milk Gill, a path heads off left by the shore. This is followed only a short way before forking right at a wider track, to acquire height while still in Burtness Wood. About 100 yards beyond a parallel wall and beck, a thin green trod, not shown on the 1:25,000 map, heads off to the right, soon leaving the wood at a stile. This superb path heads along to the left, gaining height only gradually but eventually rising more determinedly by a wall to approach Burtness Combe.

On parting company with the wall, a cairned path rises into the amphitheatre of the combe, and a similarly cairned path forks right for a direct assault on High Stile. Climbing up through heather the modest rocks of High Stile's north-east ridge are soon gained. This rib of outcrops neatly delineate the edge of the curving ridge, and though nowhere precarious, it provides an excellent route to the summit. Towards the end, and all too soon, the ridge broadens for the short pull onto the extensive top, with the highest cairn being centrally situated.

Starling Dodd

The western edge of High Stile's top proves a first class vantage point, with Bleaberry Tarn in its combe far below, and Red Pike protruding elegantly skyward. This splendid top is the next objective on the march of the great High Stile ridge, with a good path linking the two mountains. A stony descent leads quickly to a short grassy stroll before the gentlest of rises onto Red Pike's small top. To the west the grassy dome of Starling Dodd next occupies the ridge, and a thin path sets an uneventful course for it. Rather more than a mile's walk, it is soon attained and its bizarre summit cairn cannot be mistaken.

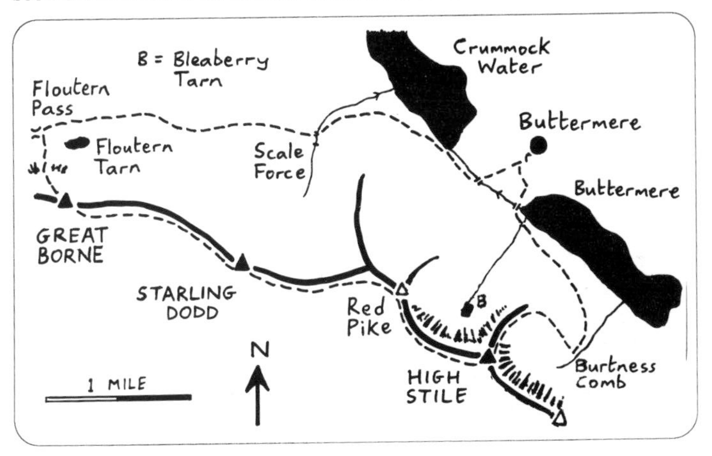

Great Borne

Just north of west Great Borne awaits, a pleasant if unexciting upland stroll leading thereto. A lovely green path is picked up in the broad depression, to hitch up with a fence for most of the climb. This twin-topped fell has its main summit, complete with Ordnance column, on the south side of the fence, which runs through a narrow trough between the tops. It is crossed by a stile to give access to the enormous cairn on the north top.

The simplest way off the top is to take up with the fence again, heading north-west to commence the steep drop of Steel Brow, between otherwise craggy slopes, to the summit of the Floutern Pass.

Turning right from the meeting of fence and path, a clear path heads away to skirt the headwaters of marshy Mosedale as it sinks away to the left. A barely discernible rise to one of the plentiful sheepfolds in this area marks the crossing of a minor watershed between Mosedale and Buttermere's valley. The path resumes only gently downwards to meet Scale Beck at the foot of Scale Force, the fall in its ravine being an impressive sight. After Floutern and Mosedale the general cheerfulness of this corner calls for a prolonged sojourn.

Beyond Scale Force the path heads off again, traversing the fellside and slowly gravitating towards the marshy environs of the head of Crummock Water. Without actually reaching the shore the path enters the woods above the alluvial plain between Crummock Water and Buttermere, and accompanies the linking Buttermere Dubs up towards the latter. Midway along it is spanned by Scale Bridge, and by crossing it the walk will end in the way it began, along a fenced lane back into the village.

The head of Buttermere from High Stile, lokking to Robinson, Hindscarth, Dale Head and fleetwith Pike

WALK 13 THE NEWLANDS ROUND

L43	**ROBINSON**	2417ft/737m
L46	**HINDSCARTH**	2385ft/727m
L42	**DALE HEAD**	2470ft/753m
L66	**HIGH SPY**	2142ft/653m

Start: Little Town (Chapel Bridge)
GR 232194 Map: NW Sheet
11 miles / 3500 feet / 5½-8 hours
Parking: off-road area on east (Little Town) side of the bridge.

Robinson

Chapel Bridge is left by the road to the west, which is itself left within yards on a narrow road to Newlands church. Bearing right at the junction here a lane makes its way up to Low High Snab, from where a path takes over to soon break out onto the open fell. At the first chance a steep climb by the wall on the right gains the improving ridge of High Snab Bank, along which a fine path gains height in style. On the crest of Blea Crags rougher terrain is briefly encountered, then the going steepens for a pull above Robinson Crags on the right. At a cairn that once promised to be the highest, the extensive summit is neared, the final strides being long ones over short turf.

Hindscarth

From Robinson's cairn Hindscarth rises across the hanging valley of Little Dale. Clearly a circuitous route must be engaged, and a good path sets the course by striking south to join and then follow a fence to the saddle of Littledale Edge. Hindscarth's top stands aside from the ridge linking Robinson and Dale Head, and instead of following

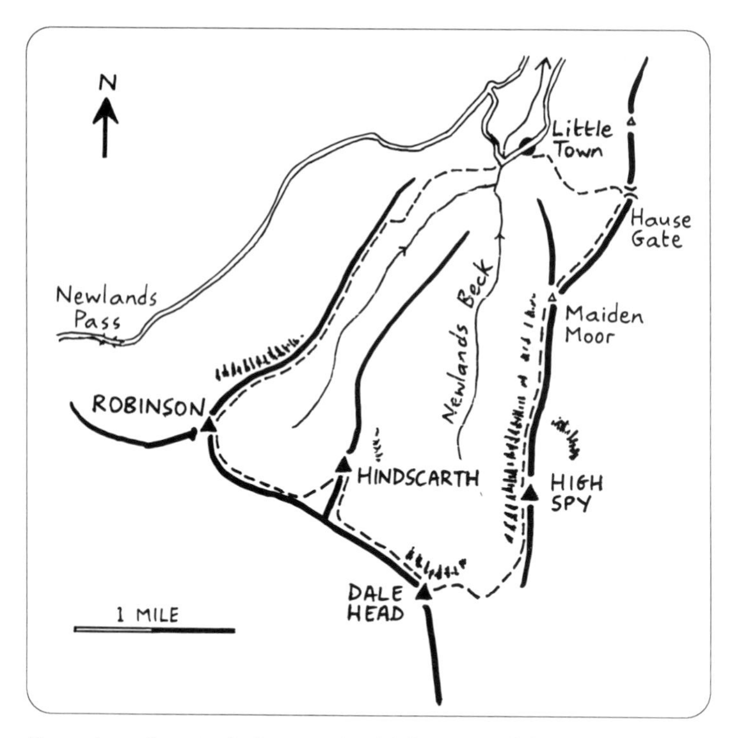

the main path up to the intervening high point and then striding north along the broad ridge to the summit, a narrow trod, a modern innovation, heads off from the saddle to slant across to the summit.

Dale Head

The transfer to Dale Head is effected by heading back along the summit ridge, forking left at a large cairn on an established slanting path to regain the senior ridge. After a short grassy promenade a more interesting pull up through the outcrops of Hindscarth Edge leads to the classy cairn, and a glimpse into the void of Newlands will explain the mountain's name.

High Spy

To the north-east across Newlands Beck is the riven wall of Eel Crags supporting the Newlands flank of High Spy, and the way onto this final mountain involves a considerable descent eastwards to Dalehead Tarn. A path sets about this simple task, the tarn soon appearing as the ground steepens, but greater interest will be found in good conditions by skirting the rim of Dalehead Crags curving to the north-east, only making for the tarn when more height has been lost. From the neighbourhood of the tarn a path completes a descent to the head of Newlands on the left, but our route takes the path unhurriedly scaling the knobbly flank of High Spy. Even at this stage of the walk the going is undemanding, and tantalising glimpses down the cliffs of Eel Crags more than occupy thoughts: the solid summit cairn hovers only yards from the brink.

Continuing north little height is lost on the broad top, even after a drop to cross aptly named Narrow Moor. Here the path divides for half a mile, the slimmer left fork opting to keep Newlands in view while crossing the top of Maiden Moor. From its highest point the path is forced north-east by a craggy flank, and rejoining the other arm a glorious descent of the ridge is enjoyed high above Derwentwater. At the saddle of Hause Gate the descent is concluded by returning allegiance to Newlands, a path swinging down to the left above old mine workings to approach the cluster of white-walled dwellings at Little Town, with Church Bridge just down the lane to the left.

WALK 14 THE COLEDALE ROUND

L31	**GRISEDALE PIKE**	2594ft/791m
	-SW Top	2424ft/739m
L37	**HOPEGILL HEAD**	2526ft/770m
	Sand Hill	2480ft/756m
L17	**GRASMOOR**	2795ft/852m
	Wandope	2532ft/772m
L21	**EEL CRAG**	2752ft/839m
	Sail	2535ft/773m
L59	**SCAR CRAGS**	2204ft/672m

Start: Braithwaite Map: NW Sheet
12 miles / 4600 feet / 6½-9½ hours
Parking: small car park on the Whinlatter road, or thoughtfully in the village.

Grisedale Pike

Braithwaite is departed by the road heading for Whinlatter Pass, and this in turn is left at a small gravel pit turned parking area on the left. A narrow path climbs to its right, soon merging into a much broader one to encounter the only stile of the day before rising through bracken onto the broad green ridge of Kinn. The entire walk is now in prospect, an impressive array of peaks hemming in the deep valley below. The immediate task is the immensely pleasurable one of gaining the top of Grisedale Pike, which now shines like a beacon ahead. After a few more hundred feet the heathery crest of Sleet How is gained, and the finest section of this east ridge draws the eager walker up through a series of outcrops that invite modest scrambles for a fitting conclusion to the ascent.

Hopegill Head

From Grisedale Pike's airy, windswept crown a well blazed path heads south-west along the slaty ridge, scaling the intervening South-west top before a major fork. The left arm sets a direct course for Coledale Hause, while the more inviting right branch clings to the rim of the Hobcarton valley. Rising with little effort above the increasingly

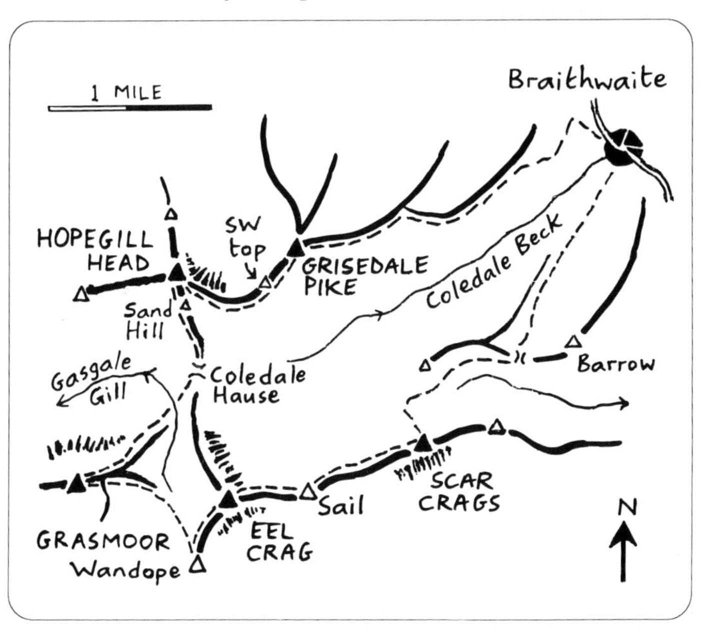

dramatic cliffs of Hobcarton Crag, it culminates on the slender summit of Hopegill Head.

Grasmoor

Having revelled in the delights of the peak of Hopegill Head, descent to Coledale Hause is a tamer affair. A broad path heads south-east over the top of Sand Hill before dropping to the grassy saddle which effectively bisects the Grasmoor massif. Although the great bulk of Grasmoor looms across the pass, there is no obvious direct route to its unseen summit. The most rewarding way forsakes the path in the pass, to at once cross Gasgale Gill as it swings to begin its tumbling descent to the right. A near pathless trek traces the clearly defined edge behind, wending up through occasional outcrops and boulders to gain the rim of the combe below Dove Crags. By this stage a thin path will have formed, and as the crags are rounded the great plateau of the summit is gained. The highest point, marked by a shapely shelter, lies some distance to the right, nearer the southern face than the flank by which ascended.

Eel Crag

From Grasmoor's top the only lines of descent that appear less than vertical involve heading eastwards again, but this time on a much used path running along the southern edge of the summit scarp, overlooking Crummock Water. This popular path declines only gently at first, but as more of Eel Crag comes into view a steeper descent is made to the upland depression between the two mountains. Here is a crossroads of paths by a brace of tiny pools, with the obvious route to Eel Crag climbing directly ahead. This pull up featureless slopes can be improved by taking a thin trod half-right from the pools to bring the top of Wandope into the day's bag. The hanging valley of Addacomb Hole divides the two mountains, and a path skirts the rim of this combe before rising left to gain Eel Crag's summit.

The top of Eel Crag is an extensive and stony plateau on which paths have made little impression: craggy slopes rim the north-east and south faces, though with care, in mist, they also act as infallible guides to the commencement of the only possible line of descent in this direction. The way off is indicated by a cairn south-east of the Ordnance column, a good path adhering to the narrow ridge which wastes no time in losing height. On encountering exposed rock hands may be required to do a steadying job, but this adds to the interest rather than to any perils. The rounded top of Sail is gained beyond a minor col, though its summit cairn stands to the left of the path and is invariably bypassed by the crowds.

Scar Crags

From Sail this high ridge takes another step nearer the valley by falling to Sail Pass, the descent thereto being rather dull after the drop off Eel Crag. Uninterrupted views over Newlands and the Vale of Keswick amply compensate, and across the pass the path makes a rapid assault on Scar Crags. The summit cairn sits at the far end of a top that is elongated but sufficiently narrow to permit views down to both sides, dramatically so to the south where cliffs and gullies seam the flank.

The return to Braithwaite is possibly the easiest descent from 2000 feet in the district, commencing with a departure from the ridge by turning down the pathless but grassy northern slopes to join the infallible course of the Stonycroft mine road. This broad track leads down to the road at Stonycroft, though after turning right along it, a direct route to Braithwaite leaves it beyond the pyramid of Outerside up to the left. As the track begins a uniform, green descent, a thin path branches left and keeps rigidly to the same contour, passing above a sheepfold and eventually meeting a similarly intentioned path rising from lower down the mine road. Together they round the flank of Stile End for the last few yards to the heathery defile of Barrow Door. Heading straight through the pass a relaxed stroll down a green swathe through bracken can be enjoyed, utilising the access road to High Coledale for the final half-mile.

South-east from Grasmoor: looking over Buttermere Moss, Fleetwith Pike and Haystacks to Gable and the Scafells

WALK 15 THE SKIDDAW GROUP

L4	**SKIDDAW**	3054ft/931m
	Skiddaw Little Man	2837ft/865m
L50	**LONSCALE FELL**	2345ft/715m

Start: Keswick Map: NW Sheet
12 miles / 3250 feet / 5½-8 hours
Parking: large car parks in the town.
Alternative start with aid of transport:
Gale Road parking area at the terminus
of the surfaced road from Applethwaite.
Grid ref 280253 (8 miles / 2450 feet).

Skiddaw

If commencing from the town centre then the route to the top of Gale Road is as follows. The market place if left by way of St. John's Street, Station Street and Station Road, crossing the Derwent and turning left into Lower Fitz Park. At its opposite corner an enclosed path escapes to emerge onto Briar Rigg, a back road. Going right along it, a bridleway known as Spooney Green Lane soon heads off to the left, crossing high above the bypass in a style far removed from its leafy nature. Once on the slopes of Latrigg this popular path rises above the trees to debouch onto the road only yards short of the car park.

At the roadhead a gate blocks the unsurfaced continuation, while immediately to the left an enclosed path begins the climb onto Skiddaw's lower flanks. Passing the Hawell Memorial the gradient increases, and there is little to excite other than the expanding retrospective view. Above the site of the long vanished refreshment hut the track scales several hundred more feet of heather slopes before gentler ground leads to the fence on Jenkin Hill. With the main peak now in view, the slopes of Little Man are rounded before recrossing the fence for the final push onto the south top. A saunter along the broad, high level ridge leads quickly to the popular summit of Skiddaw, lowest but oldest member of Lakeland's exclusive '3000' Club.

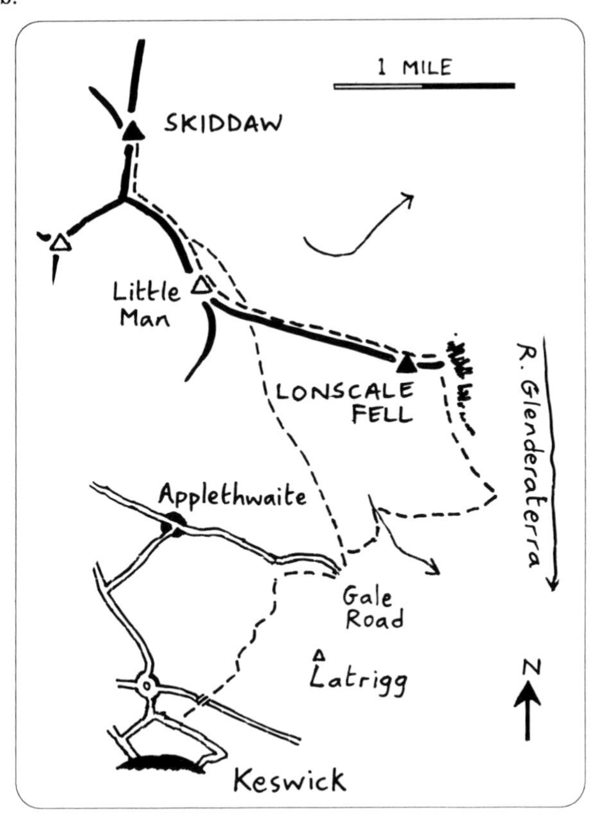

Lonscale Fell

Steps are retraced to the south summit from where the outward 'tourist' route begins its return to Keswick. In view half a mile ahead is the top of Skiddaw Little Man, which can easily be incorporated into the downward leg while avoiding treading old ground. Leaving the main path before the first encounter with the Skiddaw Forest fence a lesser path makes the short pull to the cairn, continues over its own underling Lower Man, and while enjoying the panorama over most of Lakeland, rejoins the busy route as it re-emerges through the fence.

To the bewilderment of followers of the main highway, the route onto Lonscale Fell involves going 'back' through the gate and heading directly away by the fence. The flat top of Jenkin Hill precedes a wet depression before a steady pull leads onto the broad top of Lonscale Fell. The cairn is a forlorn figure on a featureless grass plateau, and any visit to Lonscale Fell must make the brief diversion to the dramatically sited East peak, from where a craggy wall falls to the Glenderaterra far below.

Two return routes to the top of Gale Road are on offer, first and quickest being to retrace steps to a gate in the dip west of the summit, from where a path drops left to pick up the main Skiddaw path well above the road. The suggested option clings to the escarpment running south from the East peak. Remaining above the well defined tops of Lonscale Crags, the going steepens as the fence comes in from the right, and at about 1200 feet a level cross-path is met. Turning right with it through a gate, a delightful promenade ensues, sloping across the lower flank to meet the Skiddaw path just short of the road.

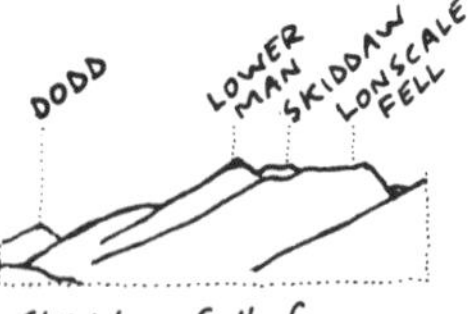

Skiddaw Fells from the Old Coach Road

WALK 16 THE CALDBECK FELLS

L62	**CARROCK FELL**	2165+ft/660+m
L63	**HIGH PIKE**	2158ft/658m
	Hare Stones	2057ft/627m
L52	**KNOTT**	2329ft/710m
L57	**GREAT CALVA**	2263ft/690m

Start: Mosedale GR 356321
Map: Pathfinder 576 (NY23/33)
13 miles/2800 feet/6-8½ hours
Parking: verge parking on the road heading west from the road through the hamlet, or off the road by the bridge to the south.

Carrock Fell

Departure from Mosedale is by the dead-end road to Swineside striking off the road through the hamlet. Within a minute it becomes unenclosed, and an immediate start to the climb is made by turning up the rough flank on the right: this initial stage of the ascent of Carrock Fell is the only part of the entire route that could remotely be described as strenuous. Life is made easier by locating a path winding up through bracken, low outcrops and rashes of stones, it being easy to be deflected by other trods. After a surprisingly effortless climb the gradient eases at a stone fold, and a strange upland plateau is exposed.

While it is possible to set a direct course north-west across the plateau, a rich tangle of vegetation and marshy ground may be sufficient reason to continue north along a thin track. This narrow trod undulates high above the crest of the line of crags defending the fell's eastern flank. If temptation to strike out half-left for the higher ground is avoided, then eventually this at times tenuous line will lead around the top of a marked depression where Further Gill Sike breaks through the craggy flank. A little further north, now climbing more above the crags, a good path is met to lead up the last short section to the cairned East top, only 400 yards from the summit cairn.

An alternative, rather more direct climb can be made from the wall

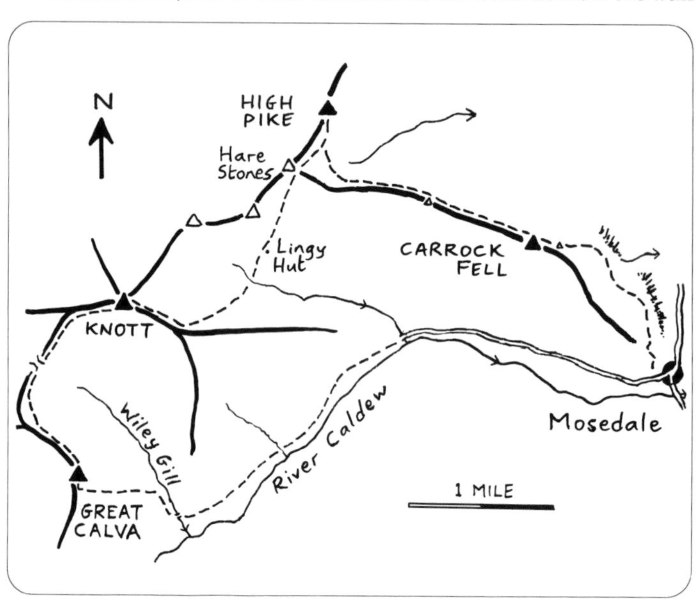

corner a little further along the road from the above starting point. Here an inviting green path slants up through the bracken, on through scree and heather, and steepens as it doubles back to the right to gain the plateau. A gentler climb then ensues rising left of an extensive rash of boulders, culminating in a straightforward rise up to the summit cairn.

High Pike

Two miles distant, High Pike is Carrock's nearest neighbour, and the way thereto is laid out in front. A reasonably clear path heads west along the wide ridge, encountering marshy ground that is soon left behind in favour of a magnificent broad path through the grass, with High Pike's cairn beckoning throughout. As the aptly named Drygill Head is neared the path forks, and the right arm swings round the head of the ravine to meet an old shooters' track to Lingy Hut. Crossing straight over, a slim path rises steadily and quickly up to High Pike's summit, where first time visitors will be duly astonished by its embellishments, most noteworthy of which is a slate seat.

Knott

Sprawling to the south-west of High Pike is the bulk of Knott. The most practical route returns to the shooters' track and follows it south, virtually over the rounded top of Hare Stones. The track ends at the Lingy Hut, now put to good use as a shelter from the elements. Beyond the hut a path takes up the reins for the stroll to Grainsgill Beck, which is charged with the awesome task of draining Miller Moss. Once across it a thin path heads half-right up a short-lived tongue, then bears further right to ascend gently over Knott's extended eastern arm. The path becomes wispish and unreliable as progress is made, but this is of little consequence during the generally dry pull up to Knott's spacious green summit.

Great Calva

From the lonely cairn on Knott the final summit, Great Calva, forms a distinctive cone almost southwards. The walk thereto, however, continues in a south-westerly direction, a thin trod developing as the slope steepens to reveal the linking col, the obvious reason for the dog-leg. A clearer path heads up the opposite slope, not waiting for the watershed before swinging left to rise through marshy surrounds to the angle of a semi-defunct fence. Its remains are then followed up to the cairn.

The old fence also acts as a guide for the descent, first by following it along the short summit ridge to the south cairn, a magnificent viewpoint for Skiddaw Forest. At this point the fence makes a sudden right-angle turn to descend the unbroken heather-clad eastern flank. At the bottom a steep bank deflects the route either left or right to join it along the short summit ridge to the south cairn, a magnificent viewpoint for Skiddaw Forest. At this point the fence makes a sudden right-angle turn to descend the unbroken heather-clad eastern flank. At the bottom a steep bank deflects the route either left or right to join Wiley Gill, where a path runs downstream to a tiny footbridge by a circular sheepfold. A good path is met here, crossing the bridge to head downstream above the substantial watercourse of the river Caldew.

This is, for Lakeland, a long walk out from the hills, but remains thoroughly enjoyable in unfrequented surroundings, even when fortified first by a shooters' track and, surprisingly, by a full surface near the defunct Carrock Mine. In the gathering gloom the road, sometimes in the company of the Caldew, offers a gentle conclusion to this lonely walk 'back o' Skidda.'

Bowscale Fell and Blencathra from Round Knott, Carrock Fell

WALK 17 THE BLENCATHRA GROUP

BLENCATHRA	2847ft/868m
Foule Crag	2772ft/845m
Bannerdale Crags	2240ft/683m
BOWSCALE FELL	2303ft/702m

Start: Mungrisdale
Map: NE & Pathfinder 576 (NY23/33)
10 miles/2750 feet/5-7 hours
Parking: roadside area opposite village hall, below the inn.

Blencathra

The village is left at the hairpin bend between the inn and the church, on a rough lane setting off from the telephone box. The lane is short-lived, and through a gate open country is entered in the company of the river Glenderamackin. The inviting track alongside heads away from the river after crossing an inflowing beck, but a thin path branches left to remain true to it. The river is followed for some two miles, squeezing between the flanks of Souther Fell and Bannerdale Crags, on what is largely a superb track on the slopes of the latter. With the target of Blencathra out of sight and mind, a sharp bend is reached and a thin path branches down to a simple bridge over the river: this can be crossed to rise up to the saddle of Mousthwaite Col, though remaining on the trusty path is rather easier.

If high winds or ice, or a general unease in exposed places dictate that Sharp Edge be omitted, then the bridge should be used, taking the slanting path up to the col and there turning right across the saddle to a path up the grassy shoulder of Scales Fell. Ignoring the path swinging right to stay parallel with the beck (the usual approach to Sharp Edge from Scales), a path ascends the broad east ridge to gain Blencathra's summit.

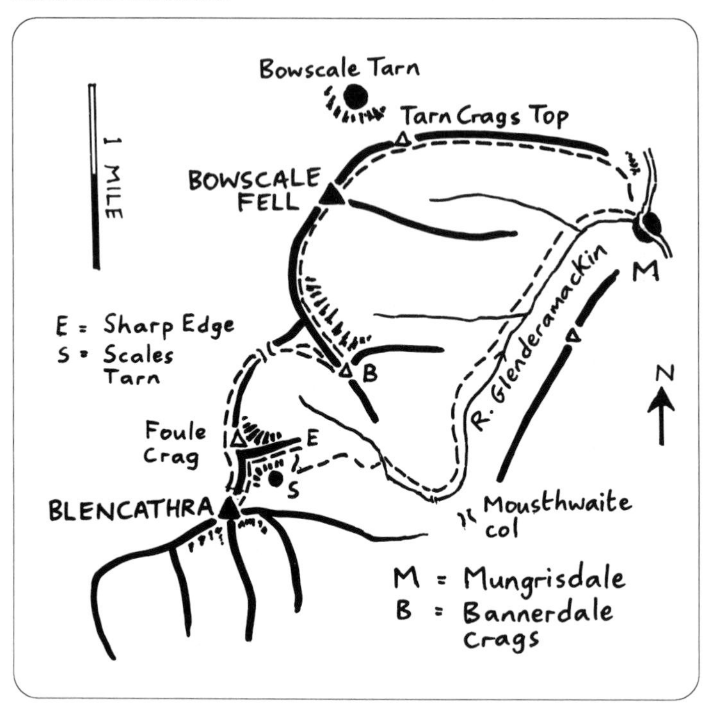

Without crossing the bridge meanwhile, the path remains its excellent self, and on rounding a corner one of the most spectacular sights in Lakeland greets the eye. This is Foule Crag, its flat top cutting away to drop sheer to the spiky ridge of Sharp Edge. Just across the beck will be seen the higher level Scales path, and at a suitable point it can be crossed to climb to that path. The path soon swings left to climb by the outflow of Scales Tarn to the water's edge, before a similarly brief pull onto the commencement of Sharp Edge.

On Sharp Edge there are no questions of route-finding, the famous knife-edge being an infallible and exhilarating guide. Those of a nervous disposition will take advantage, for the most part, of a well worn path to the north below the edge proper, but when the rocky turrets cease, all must face a fascinating little scramble up a tilted slabby face. Above it the fun ends abruptly near the top of Foule Crag, the northern top that, with the summit itself, gives the mountain its name of Saddleback. From here a much trodden path south across the eastern edge of the saddle will lead to Blencathra's meagre summit cairn. Stretching away to the west is the main ridge, and a splendid half-hour can be enjoyed by a return walk above the broken southern face to the peak of Gategill Fell Top.

Bowscale Fell

For the next stage of the journey steps are retraced to the top of Foule Crag, though this time it is simpler to stick to the crest of the broad saddle, passing a tiny tarn and a memorial cross of dazzling quartz stones. Caution is needed on leaving the cairned top of Foule Crag, for cliffs plummet immediately to north and east. A slanting path descends the slaty north-western edge to a neat little peak, the path fading but an obvious course tracing the grassy ridge to the col at the head of the Glenderamackin. On the descent to and the climb from this col, the view back to Foule Crag is positively stunning. A clear path strikes up the opposite slope, and at an early fork the left arm leads rather more directly to Bowscale Fell, though fading on the marshy ridge. By continuing uphill the right-hand path also fades in similar circumstances, but only as the rim of Bannerdale Crags is almost gained.

The cairn marking the grassy summit of Bannerdale Crags will be found just two minutes up to the right. It sits only yards from the rim of the craggy drop into the side valley of Bannerdale, and care is needed in mist. A clear path traces this edge, and is followed north around the valley head, a smashing stroll. Further north Bowscale Fell does its best to beckon, and as the path turns beyond the crags to begin to descend, it must be left in order to retain height. Now it is simply a case of making a bee-line for Bowscale Fell's grassy summit slopes, and bearing left in the marshy saddle a path re-establishes itself to give an even less strenuous rise to the summit. A shelter occupies the highest point, with the cairn a few yards further north.

From the summit a thin trod heads north-east towards the rim of Tarn Crags, from where elusive Bowscale Tarn can be viewed: a short pull to the right then leads onto Tarn Crags Top. From its cairn the return to Mungrisdale is a first-class march over the broad crest of the east ridge, a feature of which is the presence of several splendid cairns. Only at the end is steep ground encountered, taking time to locate an inviting grassy rake down to the right to avoid crags: dropping through gorse the path empties onto a rough road to re-enter the village.

Ascending Sharp Edge, Blencathra, to the top of Foule Crag

WALK 18 THE DODDS RIDGE

L47	**CLOUGH HEAD**	2381ft/726m
L16	**GREAT DODD**	2811ft/857m
L18	**STYBARROW DODD**	2765ft/843m

Start: Wanthwaite, St. John's in the Vale (B5322)
GR 316231 Map: NE Sheet
10 miles / 2900 feet / 4½-7 hours
Parking: several roadside verges. Alternative start: Legburthwaite, two miles south, where the route rejoins the road (better parking).

Clough Head

Clough Head broods ominously over the farm buildings of Wanthwaite, and it may come as a surprise to discover that a delightful, yet still direct, climb to its summit can be made. The Threlkeld-Thirlmere road is vacated when a road sign points the way to 'Matterdale, unsuitable for motors.' Known as the Old Coach Road, it climbs left of the buildings and swings left up towards Hilltop Quarries. When the accompanying wall ends, a stile in the fence gives access to the defunct workings, and a short pull leads up through spoil heaps to a broad green track. Only fifty yards to the right a parallel track, the bed of a former mineral line, is transferred to, immediately above, and from here a path sets off to climb steeply along the edge of a large quarry. From a stile at the top a thin path continues up to a tall stile over a wall and onto the open fell.

Unerringly and effortlessly a distinct sunken way rises above the wall, its twists and turns outwitting the gradient. This splendid old sledgate only expires on entering an amphitheatre above Wanthwaite Crags to the right and below the craggy scree slopes under Clough

Head's summit. At a crossroads with a sheeptrod - the right fork appearing to have been utilised by walkers - the route keeps straight on towards a cairn, and when another trod heads right only yards further, keeps straight on again on a still cairned green trod. Only yards further this appears to stop, and time should be taken to locate the clear path commencing a slanting rake up the rough flank to the right. It remains totally clear throughout, traversing the face and crossing shale shoots but always rising with ease to emerge at a cairn that marks a sudden end to the rough terrain. A thin path heads away from the cairn, but the way to the summit is a pathless stroll up the grass slopes to the left.

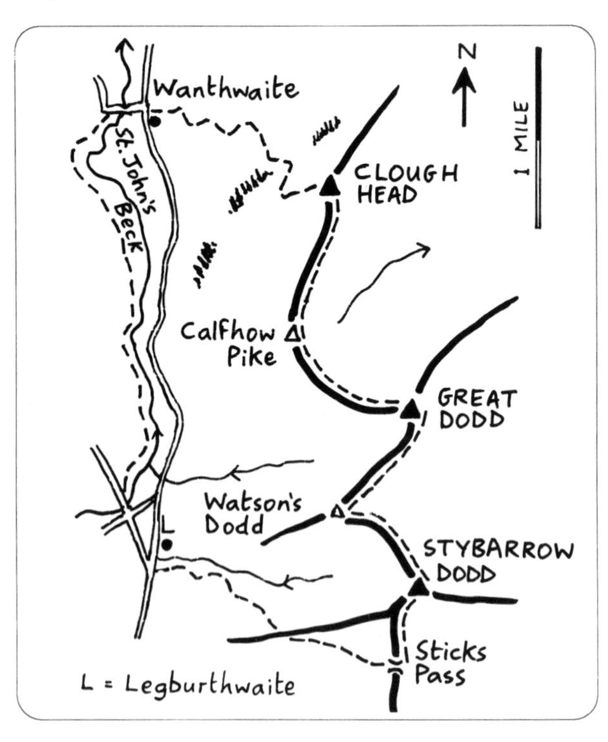

Great Dodd

Clough Head's crown is occupied by a shelter and an Ordnance column, the highlight being the prospect of Blencathra. Turning away, the dome of Great Dodd fills the ridge, and a path heads southwards for it on a grassy stroll down to Calfhow Pike. This solid tor makes an intriguing halfway point, sitting uneasily in its grassy surround. The climb to Great Dodd is uneventful, and has obviously proved sufficiently uninspiring to encourage walkers to veer right to avoid the final rise. This dubious practise is treated with the contempt it deserves by ignoring the rogue path to continue to the top. The broad summit has a cairn on the high point with a shelter to its south-east.

Stybarrow Dodd

Next summit along is Stybarrow Dodd, a similarly benign giant. The ridge dog-legs between the two, and midway encounters the minor top of Watson's Dodd. In true 'Dodds' fashion, the main path gives its cairn a wide berth, though the detour is clear and undemanding. The climb to Stybarrow Dodd is a very brief one, and, inevitably, the path performs its party piece by marginally skirting the summit. A slate boundary stone secured by a cairn marks the highest point just up to the left.

The path continues along to a cairn on the south-west top, briefly fades as the way turns south, then re-appears for a rapid descent to the top of Sticks Pass. Turning right, a good path keeps exclusively to Stybarrow Dodd's shoulder, steepest section of which is the final drop alongside Stanah Gill. The B5322 is joined as it meets the A591 at Legburthwaite, and the starting point is just under three miles to the right. Happily a relaxing return can be enjoyed without recourse to the busy road. Taking the main road towards Keswick, within half a mile, immediately after it crosses St. John's Beck, a path heads off to the right. Running below the steep flank of High Rigg, it either shadows or runs within a field's length of the beck all the way to the next road crossing: a right turn here, over Wanthwaite Bridge, leads back to the road at the walk's start.

WALK 19 THE GLENRIDDING FELLS

L9	**CATSTYCAM**	2919ft/890m
L3	**HELVELLYN**	3116ft/950m
	Lower Man	3034ft/925m
	White Side	2831ft/863m
L11	**RAISE**	2896ft/883m
L58	**SHEFFIELD PIKE**	2214ft/675m

Start: Glenridding Map: NE Sheet
12 miles / 4000 feet / 6-9 hours
Parking: large car park in centre.

Catstycam

Glenridding is left by the rough road alongside the beck from the shops. At Rattlebeck Bridge the beck is forsaken for the access road rising left to Miresbeck, continuing up the pasture above to gain the open fell. Shunning the path climbing by the beck, a right turn sees the start of a long, level mile under Birkhouse Moor, with Glenridding Beck down to the right and Sheffield Pike, the day's final top, rising out of the devastation of the old Greenside lead mines. Rounding a corner the environs of the mine workings are left behind, and the beck is rejoined at a small footbridge above an impressive waterfall display. It is here that an alternative start up the Greenside road from the car park and through the various former mine buildings meets the prescribed route, which declines to cross the bridge but remains on the south side of the beck.

Disinclined to gain any discernible height, the path contents itself with a first view of Catstycam, which now dominates the scene and occupies all thoughts. Beyond a sheepfold at a confluence, a simple bridge carries the path over Red Tarn Beck from where the climb begins above its bank. Issuing from the tarn of that name, this lively watercourse guides the path unerringly, albeit a trifle moistly at the end, to its shore. The best plan, however, is to leave the path as the pull eases above a waterfall, and make a direct assault on the upper 700 or so feet of Catstycam's eastern shoulder. It is mostly grassy, and a cairned path can be located to assist in the stonier upper stages to gain the distinct peak of the summit.

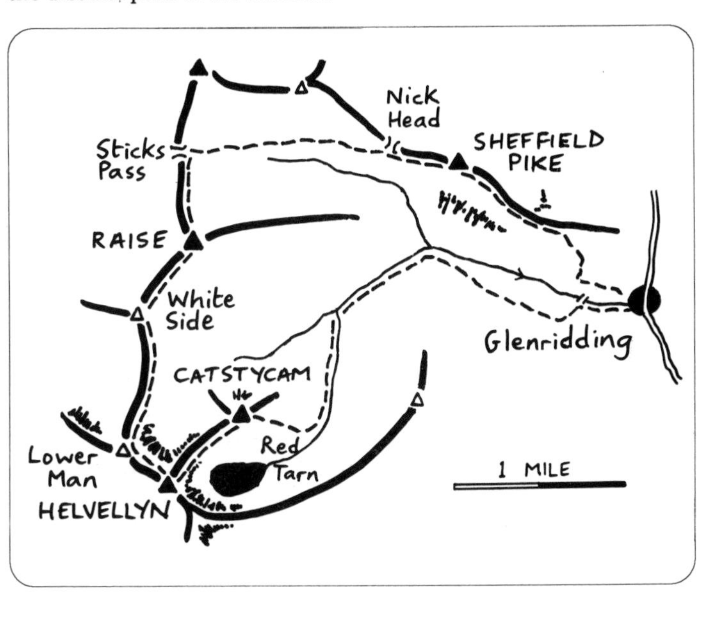

Helvellyn

From Catstycam's airy perch the route onto Helvellyn can be in no doubt, for the course of Swirral Edge assaulting the rugged east face is worthy of a prolonged appraisal. With the chilly waters of Red Tarn down to the left, a rapidly accomplished descent precedes an exhilarating confrontation with Helvellyn's less famous 'edge.' Although shorter lived than its more illustrious counterpart across the tarn,

Swirral Edge has the decided advantage of a far more solid rock scramble to attain the summit plateau. Those averse to employing hands during the ascent can weave to either side of the arête proper, and the whole episode should only encounter potential danger in ice or very strong winds. From the cairned top a broad path runs above the escarpment to the Ordnance column, a little beyond which is a lacklustre cairn and, below that, a well patronised shelter.

Raise

From Helvellyn's summit the way lies to the north, and a broad highway, much inferior to tracing the escarpment, bypasses the top of Swirral Edge and aims for the lofty saddle in front of Lower Man. This subsidiary top is breasted before an enjoyable descent of its north rib marks the transfer to less dramatic surroundings, though the aspect of Catstycam across Brown Cove is superb. Across a col the broad path, choked with cairns, rises to the summit cairn on White Side. Raise waits beyond the next, wider col, in which a path forking right provides a quick return to the valley. A gentle slope climbs to its stubbly summit, located at the far end of the felltop.

Sheffield Pike

North of Raise the mighty barrier of the Helvellyn range drops to the Sticks Pass at 2420ft before continuing in tamer but still lofty fashion over the Dodds ridge. After the short amble down to the pass, however, this walk heads for home, though one further peak still awaits. Turning right from the summit of the pass, a path descends to the amphitheatre of the drained Sticks Reservoir, a redundant morass that once served the lead mines immediately below. Sheffield Pike is clearly in view ahead, eastwards, and when the path has skirted the basin of the old reservoir, the Sticks Pass route is vacated. On turning sharply right along the line of the former dam, just as it draws level with a row of spoil heaps, a profusion of small cairns identify the precise point where a thin path makes its exit to the left. If the clouds are down at this stage then it might be better to save Sheffield Pike to be tackled on its own on a better day, and on this occasion simply continue down the pass.

Wending its way up between grassy knolls, the path soon escapes the mining area and within a few minutes and two hundred feet of re-ascent the juicy saddle of Nick Head is reached. This is the link between Sheffield Pike and its higher neighbour Stybarrow Dodd, visited in Walk 18. At the small cairn on Nick Head a distinct path heads north-east to begin an immediate descent to Glencoyne, and should not be mistaken for the wispy path commencing a steady pull up to Sheffield Pike's cairn.

Two less than obvious paths head east from the summit, the clearer one aiming more to the right over marshy terrain. The key is to gain the far south-eastern corner of this dreary upland, aiming to the right of an iron boundary post. Here is a distinct edge, with substantial crags lining the Glenridding flank, and sizeable outcrops immediately beneath the iron post. Once located, a thin but obvious path picks its way down the south-east ridge. Decorated with tracts of heather this is a memorable route, with a glorious panorama over Ullswater and Patterdale's valley backed by Lakeland's easternmost fells. The descent is halted at a neat defile opposite Glenridding Dodd: the final stage is down a path to the right, romping through bracken to emerge onto the Greenside mine road at the terraces of Upper Glenridding, thence following it down to the village.

Helvellyn and Lower Man from the north

WALK 20 THE GRISEDALE FELLS

L15	**DOLLYWAGGON PIKE**	2814ft/858m
L45	**SEAT SANDAL**	2414ft/736m
L19	**SAINT SUNDAY CRAG**	2758ft/841m

Start: Patterdale Map: NE Sheet
11½ miles / 4000 feet / 6-9 hours
Parking: car park in village, and a larger one in Glenridding.

Dollywaggon Pike

The day begins with an extended 3 mile walk-in along the green floor of Grisedale. For those unfamiliar with this famous entry to the hills, the valley's access road leaves the A592 at the Glenridding end of the village, past the church but just before the road crosses Grisedale Beck. The narrow surfaced lane climbs high above the beck before levelling out with it at a junction of departing farm roads. Either can be taken, but the most direct is the one remaining on the south side of the dale.

Rising impressively ahead, with ample time to be appraised, is the neat peak of Dollywaggon Pike: it is succeeded on the right by rounded High Crag, flat-topped Nethermost Pike, and Striding Edge hemming in the valley. After the surfaced road branches off to Braestead, a long, level track continues, and not until the pastures and plantations are left behind does a short climb ensue, above a gorge secreting Grisedale Falls. Just above it the path eventually crosses Grisedale Beck by a footbridge, merges with the other valley path and then makes the short ascent to the climbing hut of Ruthwaite Lodge.

At Ruthwaite Lodge the beaten track is discarded in favour of a slender green path zig-zagging up through bracken, well to the left of the spritely Ruthwaite Beck and a parallel stream. When the steepness recedes the slight path slants right towards the sidestream: as the amphitheatre of Ruthwaite Cove is not the objective, the stream need not be crossed. Two means of gaining Dollywaggon Pike's east ridge, known as the Tongue, now present themselves. The first involves contouring left to the crest of Spout Crag, prominent during the climb, the second is to rise with the beck to then slope across to a conspicuous grass gully farther up, the final pull being steep but undemanding.

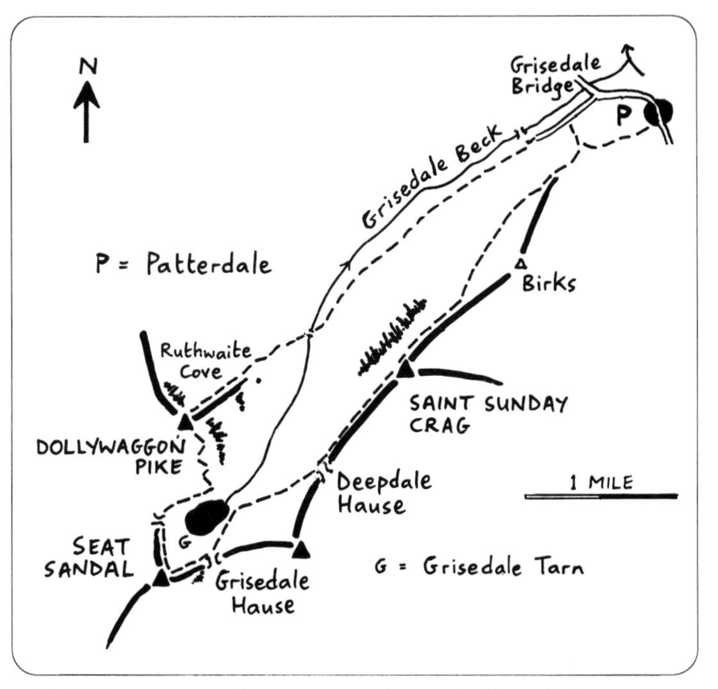

Knobbly outcrops take over as an increasingly stylish ascent unfolds. As the ridge narrows a thin path, superfluous in this upper stage, materialises to claim the summit of the mountain: on this approach there is little chance of missing the cairn. Despite its intimidating look from the valley, the whole of this route up the Tongue can be accomplished almost with hands in pockets, yet its undeniable character must offset any inferiority complex brought on by its proximity to Helvellyn.

Seat Sandal

The next objective seems an unlikely target, but is really the natural watershed progression. By descending south-west from the cairn a well blazed track from Helvellyn down to Grisedale Tarn will be quickly picked up, and by turning left the zig-zag drop to the foot of the tarn soon commences. In clear weather this busy track can be shunned by setting a direct course for the wide col between Dollywaggon Pike and Seat Sandal. A crumbling wall may be found to point the way as height is lost, and it in fact returns on the facing slope of Seat Sandal.

The alternative is to remain on the zig-zags until nearer the tarn, then break off right to pick up a narrow path that runs from the outflow to the col high above Dunmail Raise. From it the climb by the old wall is grassy and quickly accomplished, the wall being a sure guide as it runs to within a few yards of the summit cairn on the broad top. Seat Sandal provides a welcome break from the crowds on the paths at its foot, and also offers a fine panorama of the Lakeland skyline westwards.

Saint Sunday Crag

The wall on Seat Sandal is also useful in indicating the way off, for it makes a sharp turn on the summit to head east, soon commencing a steep drop - during which it should be kept on the right - to the crest of Grisedale Hause. Here a further loss of height must be undergone by taking the path down to the foot of Grisedale Tarn. Without crossing the outflow, the main path is vacated in favour of locating one that begins sketchily to rise steadily right towards Deepdale Hause, and in the obvious direction of St. Sunday Crag. A well sited cairn offers itself as a guide, and within a couple of minutes a clearly defined path should be underfoot. This excellent path slants up beneath Fairfield's rough flank with great economy of effort to gain the Fairfield-St. Sunday Crag ridge at its very saddle: this is Deepdale

Hause, rarely used as such. Prominent throughout the walk, St. Sunday Crag is at last firmly underfoot, and by turning left a surprisingly long but again undemanding climb up the ridge leads, in the fullness of time, to the summit cairn.

The way off St. Sunday Crag involves tracing the sketchy but cairned path heading slightly east of north towards the edge of the cliffs above Grisedale, where a cairn marks a celebrated viewpoint for Ullswater. Swinging north-east the path becomes infallible, descending through the occasional outcrops of the north-east ridge to a junction on a rather marshy depression. Here the main path bears slightly left, crossing the flank of subsidiary top Birks while losing very little further height.

Easy gradients continue high above Grisedale until the path arrives at a wall on Thornhow End. Beyond it the final stage of the descent is a well worn, winding path down to a stile. Here a choice of finishes awaits: a left turn leads directly onto the Grisedale lane high above the beck, while to the right a track contours round through the trees of Glemara Park. A continuing path emerges behind the Patterdale Hotel, either turning left for it, or keeping on a little further past Mill Moss for the other licensed premises, the White Lion.

Ullswater and Birk Fell (Place Fell) from St. Sunday Crag's North-east ridge

WALK 21 PLACE FELL

L64 **PLACE FELL** 2155ft/657m

Start: Sandwick (GR 423195)
Map: NE Sheet $5^{1/2}$ miles / 1900 feet / 3-4 hours
Parking: Very limited at or just before Sandwick. The suggestion is to park a car on Martindale Hause,and follow the path to Sandwick by way of Hallin Bank and Bridge End.

From the handful of buildings at Sandwick the walk starts on the wide track heading west along the foot of the open fell, bound for Patterdale. On this walk, however, it must be vacated before it gains Ullswater's shore. The break comes after crossing a bridge over lively Scalehow Beck, whose waterfalls will have already aroused interest. After the short rise to the wall corner beyond the bridge, a thin trod runs along through bracken on the left, soon climbing a little to draw level with the falls. Just above, the path fades, and the object is to gain the low ridge up to the right, emanating from Birk Fell. This is achieved by climbing through bracken up to low outcrops on the right, then working across further right to locate a tenuous trod that climbs between the minor outcrops of the well defined ridge-end. With Ullswater far below, this section soon terminates at a splendidly sited beacon on Low Birk Fell, prominent near the start of the walk.

From the beacon the upland stage of the climb can be surveyed, the curving arm of Birk Fell connecting with the higher ground of the summit further back to the left. A delectable trod sets forth over the ridge's grassy undulations, past twin ruinous folds to reach a short, steep climb onto Birk Fell proper. A cairn offers a greeting on the crest of the ridge, but the real top is set back to the right farther on, and is bypassed by the path. Beyond a marshy depression, a cairn stands above a groove rising from the steep flank on the right: this heralds the arrival of a direct climb from Ullswater, and united, the two ways form a clearer green path making for the summit. Rising beneath the cairned top of The Knight, the path becomes clearer still for the final short pull onto the felltop. A cairn and an impressively perched Ordnance column vie for supremacy.

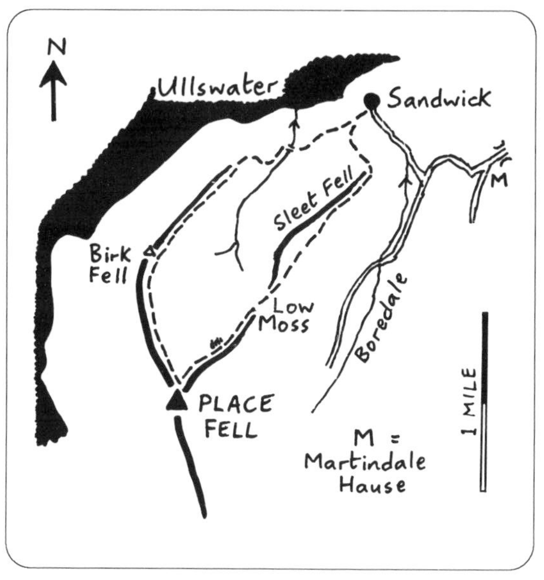

Two major paths depart the summit, one south to Boredale Hause, the other north-east past a tarn. This is the way to Sandwick, along the crest of Hart Crag and descending pleasantly to a sheepfold on Low Moss. A clear path bearing left after the fold provides the quickest and easiest way down, but in good weather higher ground can be savoured as long as possible by remaining on the inviting path straight ahead. As it swings round beneath the grassy alp of High Dodd up to the left, this delectable green swathe offers another exit to the valley, in the form of a superlative path winding down through bracken on the right.

Where the path sets off for the valley, the ridge can be used still longer by continuing on, the broad path soon becoming a thin trod after the junction. It maintains this fashion on or near the grassy ridge top of Sleet Fell to terminate abruptly at a substantial cairn above a sudden drop to Howe Grain. Here it is necessary to go left with a well collapsed wall, which sets the course for the last stage of the descent. Dropping steeply with the mound that is its only remnant lower down, the steep bracken-covered flank meets another path linking Low Moss and Sandwick, and the finish is just along it to the right.

The summit, looking to the northern High Street range

Ullswater and Hallin Fell from Low Birk Fell

WALK 22 THE MARTINDALE FELLS

L60	**LOADPOT HILL**	2201ft/671m
	Wether Hill	2207ft/673m
L25	**HIGH RAISE**	2631ft/802m
	Rampsgill Head	2598ft/792m
L22	**HIGH STREET**	2716ft/828m
L55	**REST DODD**	2283ft/696m

Start: Martindale (Old Church)
GR 434184 Map: NE Sheet
15 miles / 3250 feet / 6½-10 hours
Parking: tidily, just off the road.

Loadpot Hill

From the church a path heads up through bracken, climbing right of a big enclosure at the top of which it begins a gentle slant across the flank of Steel Knotts. The top of the ridge is met after passing through a wall, which is then followed along the broadening ridge. After bypassing the knoll of Brownthwaite Crag the thin path swings left under Gowk Hill to run along to meet the wall again. Passing at once through a gateway to two ruined huts, the path climbs by a tiny beck before crossing it.

Immediately over the beck the now level path is left in order to follow the beck up, passing through a marshy area before rising more confidently to locate a well defined groove. This zig-zags tidily up and only fades as the gradient eases, by which time the High Street Roman road is only yards further. A mile to the left is the dome of Loadpot Hill, a visit to which calls for a retracing of steps back to this point. The detour is quickly accomplished, the Roman road being used as far as

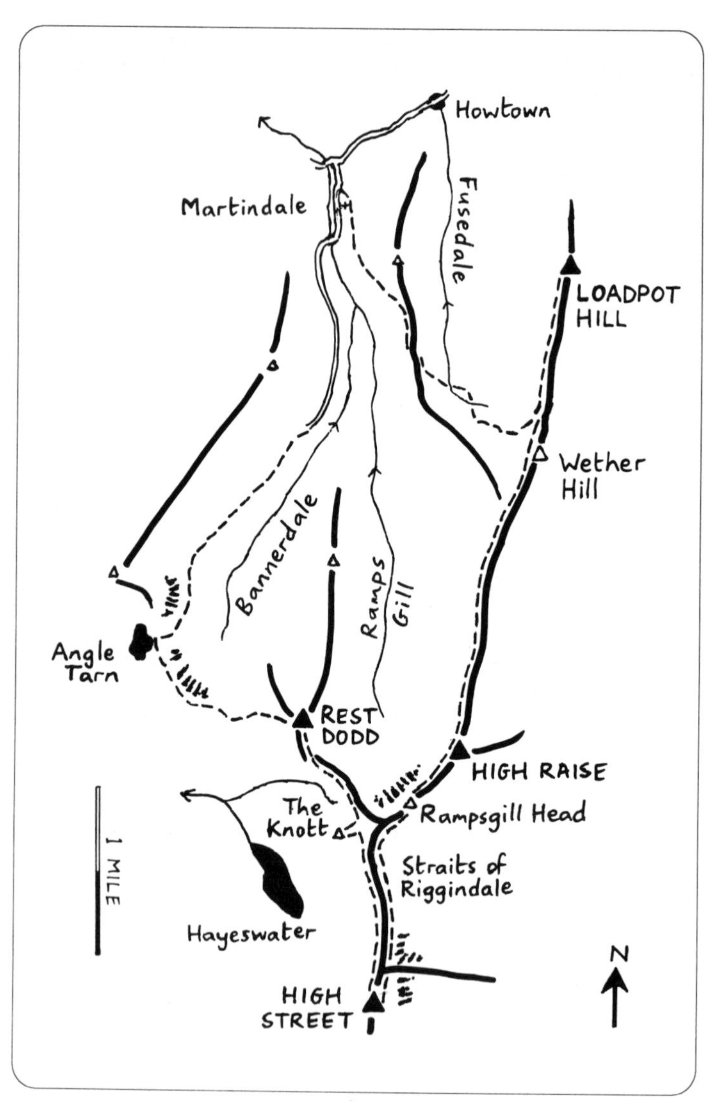

Howtown
Martindale
Fusedale
LOADPOT HILL
Wether Hill
Bannerdale
Ramps Gill
Angle Tarn
REST DODD
HIGH RAISE
The Knott
Rampsgill Head
1 MILE
Straits of Riggindale
Hayeswater
N
HIGH STREET

the scant ruin of Lowther House, a former shooting lodge. Here a path climbs directly onto the broad top, a small cairn and a large Ordnance column, 50 yards apart, marking the summit.

High Raise

Back on the Roman road steps now turn south, skirting Wether Hill's twin tops - the second being regarded as marginally higher - and passing the point where the ridge was joined, to descend slightly to meet a wall coming up from Rampsgill. After a short spell in its company the path breaks off right to accompany a fence over the cairned tops of Red Crag and Raven Howe before a marked pull up towards High Raise. Soon after the wall's return, both it and the fence head back into Rampsgill, and the path continues onto High Raise. The summit cairn is located a few yards to the left of the path's highest point.

High Street

The great whaleback of High Street is the next objective, and the Roman road is the means of linking the two. In the saddle below High Raise the path forks, the old road taking the gentle left arm while the right fork has been trodden to prominence by modern fellwalkers. As there is little to choose, it pays to opt for the right fork, and thereby include Rampsgill Head in the day's outing. Despite a broad top it offers splendid views down into Rampsgill, though it is best avoided in bad weather as that face is close to hand and particularly steep. Although both paths falter, by continuing south the wide path around the rim of Riggindale and out to Kidsty Pike cannot be missed.

Turning right along the path, it descends gently to the Straits of Riggindale. This narrow saddle is the springboard for the detour to High Street, and a choice of routes permits a varied return from the top. Most direct is the path accompanying the wall, foolproof but dull, while most enjoyable is the least used, which skirts the Riggindale edge until striking for the top on reaching a cairn above the Long Stile ridge. The third option is the well blazed course of the Roman road: this steers well clear of the summit, and is best used for the return.

Rest Dodd

On returning to the Straits the route resumes by forking left on the wallside path. At a sharp angle in it the path swings away, but for the sake of an additional minute, the wall can be followed up to the left to visit the rounded top of the Knott. The same wall proves an infallible guide to similarly rounded but better defined Rest Dodd to the north, descending to be crossed by the main path then crossing a marshy dip to climb to within a short distance of Rest Dodd's top. The worst of the damp can be side-stepped by returning to the wall corner below the Knott's summit, then crossing the path to take an obvious line above the steep drop into Rampsgill. From the saddle either the wall can be rejoined for the climb, or the edge of the Rampsgill face traced up to the grassy, triple-cairned top.

The return to the start begins by again joining the Patterdale-High Street path by striking west from the top, the path coming into view several hundred feet below: the wall also serves as a guide. Turning right along it, minor outcrops are encountered above Satura and Buck Crags before reaching Angle Tarn. When level with the main island the path is vacated by crossing over the low grassy saddle on the right, and a thin path will be located turning down to the left in the company of the wall enclosing the Martindale Deer Forest at the head of Bannerdale.

After a spell by the wall the path breaks off for an enjoyable traverse beneath Heck Crag, rejoining the wall once the rougher environs subside. Departure from this magnificent valley head is along a gem of a green path through bracken, arriving at the farm of Dale Head in fine style. Here a surfaced road takes over, and its traffic-free course is followed back to the church through the valley of Howe Grain in deepest Martindale.

WALK 23 THE FAIRFIELD GROUP

	Heron Pike	2037ft/621m
	Great Rigg	2513ft/766m
L12	**FAIRFIELD**	2863ft/873m
	Hart Crag	2696ft/822m
L30	**DOVE CRAG**	2598ft/792m
L35	**RED SCREES**	2545ft/776m

Start: Ambleside Map: NE & SE Sheets
14 miles / 4200 feet / 7-10 hours
Parking: main car park at north end of town.

Fairfield

A stroll through the parkland of Rydal Hall makes a leisurely preamble to a lengthy tramp over high fells. It is reached by heading north on the main road out of town, leaving it through large gates by a lodge on the right. The broad drive extends for a full mile, during which time the cirque of fells rimming the head of Rydal's valley present themselves prior to their traverse. At the hall a well sign-posted path is channelled between buildings to emerge onto a lane above Rydal church.

Climbing begins in earnest as the lane rises past Rydal Mount, and at once loses its surface. Through a gateway the path turns off to the left, a steep pull between walls being cushioned by skilfully restored zig-zags and rapidly unfolding views. Emerging onto open fell the well engineered path resumes its skyward progress, and easy climbing soon earns a respite above Nab Scar, after crossing the final stile for many a long mile.

From the cairn above Nab Scar steadier climbing soon brings the

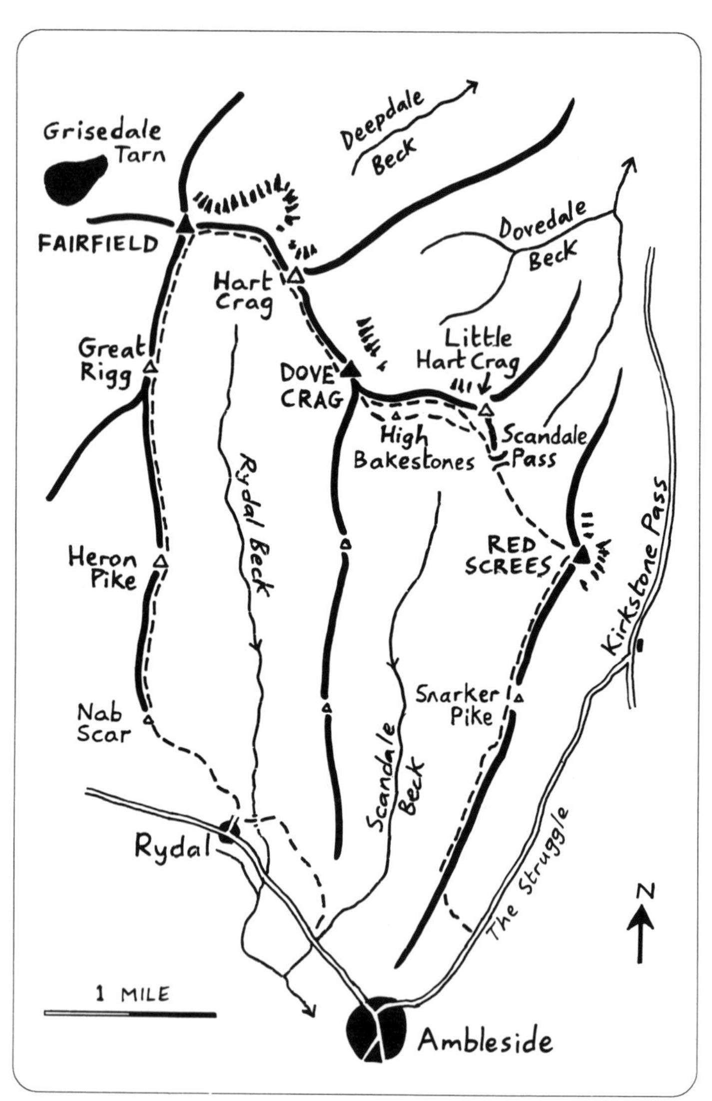
Grisedale Tarn
Deepdale Beck
FAIRFIELD
Dovedale Beck
Hart Crag
Great Rigg
Little Hart Crag
DOVE CRAG
High Bakestones
Scandale Pass
Rydal Beck
Heron Pike
RED SCREES
Kirkstone Pass
Snarker Pike
Nab Scar
Scandale Beck
Rydal
The Struggle
N
1 MILE
Ambleside

two summits of Heron Pike underfoot, the higher northern one rising beyond a saddle and bypassed by the main path. Simple fellwalking along a broad, undulating ridge precedes a keener pull to the sprawling cairn on Great Rigg, the final section being a pleasant stony climb. The great mass of Fairfield now broods unobstructed across a minor depression, from where the path rises unfailingly to the summit plateau of the parent fell. Paths have not taken well to this stony top, and if unfavourable weather sets in, he who does not already know Fairfield must exercise particular caution: to north and east the summit is rimmed by cliffs.

Dove Crag

On a good day a rewarding lunch break can be enjoyed from one of innumerable vantage points overlooking the cliffs and gullies around the head of Deepdale, and these can be located during the next stage of the walk. An improving path heads a good hundred yards south-east from the highest point to round the head of a scree-filled gully before striking east en route for Hart Crag. In clear weather only, the path should be vacated in order to appreciate the rugged scenery to the left.

The main path and the explorer's route will meet up after turning south to the outcrops above Scrubby Crag, from where only a short drop leads onto the col with Hart Crag. It is but a brief climb to this roughest top of the day, it being necessary to break off the main highway in order to gain one of the identical twin summits up to the right. From the farthest one the domed top soon breaks away, and the path clambers down through a field of boulders. In the ensuing depression a wall is met, and this steers the path up to the spacious summit of Dove Crag, whose cairn stands a few yards east of the wall.

Red Screes

By now inextricably linked, path and wall head south from Dove Crag, clinging to the watershed of the ridge that ends above Rydal Park and Ambleside. Having completed three-quarters of the celebrated Fairfield Horseshoe, the route now opts for a new watershed, and within minutes of leaving Dove Crag turns east to shadow a ruinous fence down the eastern shoulder to skirt Bakestones Moss. By continuing a little farther south before branching off, an alternative path will be picked up, which pays a visit to the prominent stone men on High Bakestones before descending to a less evasive encounter with the moss.

The paths merge above a wall corner, under the castellated top of Little Hart Crag, and thoughts now turn to the bulk of Red Screes waiting patiently across Scandale Pass. The main path accompanies the wall down to the grassy saddle of the pass and most of the way up the opposite slope, a climb that can seem longer than it really is at this stage of the walk. When the wall gives up the ghost, the gradient relents and the extensive top of Red Screes has been gained. Adorned by a large cairn, an Ordnance column and a rather more decorative tarn, the highest point is located to the east of the plateau, and perched above an alarming plunge to the Kirkstone Pass.

From Red Screes it is time to turn for home, and so begins the descent of its south ridge. Initially heading left of the tarn, a good path forms to run along to a cairn above the brink of Raven Crag, then continues down through the sparing contours of the ridge. Not only is this a remarkably effortless descent, it has the good fortune to possess a gem of a path. After a slight narrowing of the ridge to produce Snarker Pike (cairn over the wall), the path is soon ushered to the right by another wall, and from a stile begins a march down a green lane to end all green lanes. In the fullness of time it emerges onto the Struggle, from Ambleside up to Kirkstone, and the final stretch leads down into the town, emerging opposite the car park.

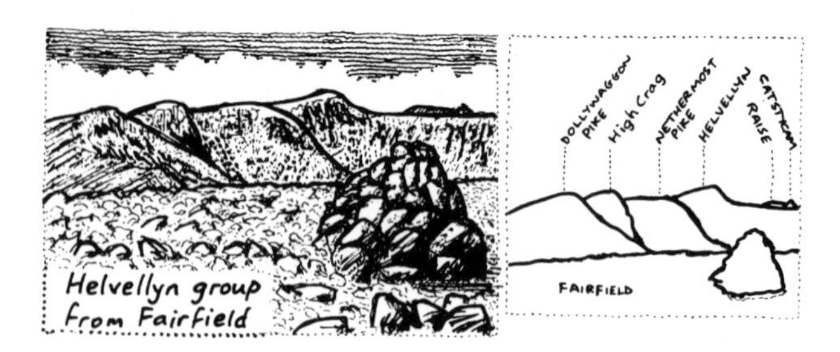

Helvellyn group from Fairfield

WALK 24 THE TROUTBECK FELLS

	Yoke	2316ft/706m
L41	**ILL BELL**	2483ft/757m
	Froswick	2362ft/720m
	Thornthwaite Crag	2572ft/784m
L38	**CAUDALE MOOR**	2503ft/763m

Start: Troutbeck (Church, on A592)
GR 413028 Map: SE Sheet
12 miles / 3600 feet / 6-8½ hours
Parking: limited parking up the lane by Church Bridge, or by the school.

Ill Bell

From Church Bridge the main road is followed briefly south before turning off up the rough lane on the left: this is the start of the Garburn Road, once an important route into Kentmere. After a steep pull it swings left and follows an unswerving course to gradually gain height above the Troutbeck valley, and only after a considerable time is the top of the pass neared. While a path heads off to the left from the gate on the very top, another strikes off a littler earlier to escape some of the marshy ground that prevails hereabouts.

Whether followed initially or not, the wall on the right soon becomes a close companion on the steady climb. When it parts company at a stile, a steeper section is quickly completed and the going eases up again to arrive at a fork: the left path opts to contour to avoid the summit of Yoke, while that on the right does the honourable thing and pays it a visit. Now the walk is well and truly on the tops, and from Yoke the wide path heads north across a depression to climb to the

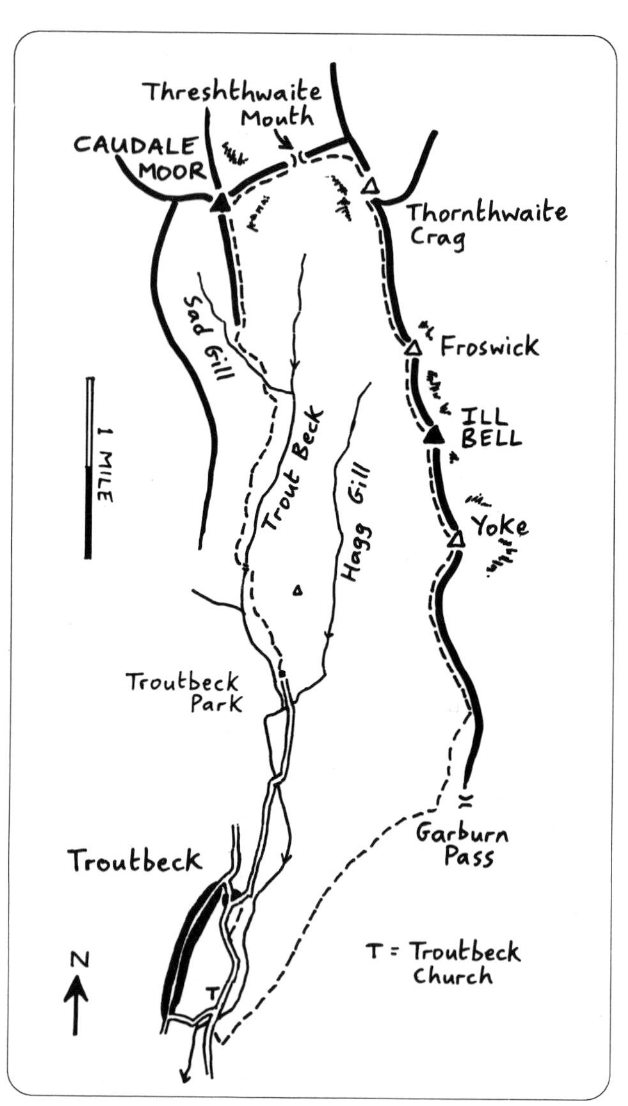
Threshthwaite
Mouth
CAUDALE
MOOR
Thornthwaite
Crag
Sad Gill
Froswick
1 MILE
ILL
BELL
Trout Beck
Hagg Gill
Yoke
Troutbeck
Park
Garburn
Pass
Troutbeck
N
T
T = Troutbeck
Church

summit of Ill Bell, an attractive top bedecked with shapely cairns.

Caudale Moor

Ill Bell's favourite of its two satellites is Froswick, just over half a mile to the north and made in its own likeness. Destined to forever stand in the shadow of its parent fell, it nevertheless well repays the effort of a visit. This involves ignoring the ubiquitous contouring path in favour of following the main path up the grassy ridge, skirting the impressive drops into the upper Kentmere valley to gain its tidy summit.

From Froswick the path effects a rapidly accomplished descent followed by a long, gradual rise to the northern terminus of this lofty ridge between Troutbeck and Kentmere. Part way up the protracted climb it is important to keep left at a major fork at a forlorn iron post in order to attain the summit of Thornthwaite Crag. It is marked in unique style by an immense monolith known as the Beacon: with a wall running alongside, this is a pre-eminent lunch halt. Though really only a shoulder of High Street, Thornthwaite Crag occupies a strategic position at the meeting place of various ridges. For this reason it is essential to locate the correct way off, which on this occasion is north-west, towards the great bulk of Caudale Moor.

The two mountains are joined at the defile of Threshthwaite Mouth, not in view from the summit but soon all too evident, several hundred feet below. The path thereto remains with the crumbling wall curving steadily north-west from the Beacon, the ground soon steepening into a stony, zig-zag descent to the pass. Only the briefest respite from the gradients is offered at this deep col, the ensuing climb onto Caudale Moor, in the company of the same wall, being very immediate, very steep, yet very enjoyable thanks to the more solid rock. When the climb relents a long, easy walk deals with the final two hundred feet: almost at a wall junction the main path cuts the final corner and bears left to attain the summit cairn, which itself stands just in front of a crosswall that has seen better days.

The fell's name is an apt one, for although it has its share of craggy flanks, its summit is an extensive, moor-like plateau. At this stage of the walk Troutbeck remains as distant as it has ever been, and the most direct route heads south from the cairn, shadowing the aforementioned wall. An attractive ridge forms almost at once, being grassy, well defined and gloriously free of paths. The wall remains as company until a demise which it shares with the ridge itself. At a T-junction the facing wall offers no means of crossing other than a careful climb in the corner. If this goes against the grain, then the easy answer is to turn left and accompany it down towards the infant Trout Beck, picking up, only yards before the stream, the rarely trodden path down from Threshthwaite Mouth.

In clear weather the crossing of the wall junction leads to an interesting descent. Keeping straight ahead to meet Sad Gill as it prepares for a lively fall to the valley, it can be followed down through several minor outcrops, care being needed where a narrow and potentially lethal ravine is born to its left as the valley is neared. It is better to cross the beck before an inflowing parallel beck joins it near the bottom, and to pick up a thin green track on its opposite bank. As the ground levels out on the valley floor the descent intercepts the path coming down from Threshthwaite Mouth, running parallel with but now further away from Trout Beck.

The main beck is now followed downstream, at a respectable distance in order to avoid marshy ground. In time it is crossed at a stone bridge before continuing down to pass through Troutbeck Park farm and out along its seemingly endless access road back to Troutbeck. As it climbs to meet the main road, a corner can be cut by turning left along an enclosed bridleway. Once on the main road, the church is just down to the left.

WALK 25 THE LONGSLEDDALE FELLS

L61	**TARN CRAG**	2178ft/664m
L51	**BRANSTREE**	2339ft/713m
L34	**HARTER FELL**	2552ft/778m
	Kentmere Pike	2394ft/730m

Start: Sadgill, Longsleddale
GR 483056 Map: SE Sheet
9 miles / 3200 feet / 4½-7 hours
Parking: at the road end, Sadgill Bridge. There is no parking across the bridge, and care should be taken not to block the unmade road continuing up the valley.

Tarn Crag

From the end of the surfaced road at Sadgill Bridge, the route sets forth in style along the wide, enclosed former quarry road that heads zealously into the upper reaches of Longsleddale. Beyond the imposing mass of Buckbarrow Crag, on the right, the old road starts to climb above the tumbling waters of the infant river Sprint, and the walk remains on it until it passes through a gate to wander free. Just ahead is the former Wrengill Quarry on Harter Fell, past which the track continues, to be met again on the crest of the Gatescarth Pass.

From the gate, however, it is time to break sweat by striking up the grassy slope to the right, first by a wall and soon with a fence for company. When the fence terminates at a junction, the summit of Tarn Crag can be gained by continuing a little further uphill to skirt the marshy depression on the right, then swinging right to reach the broad top. The presence of a stone survey tower, a relic of the

Haweswater pipeline construction, ensures this can only be Tarn Crag's summit.

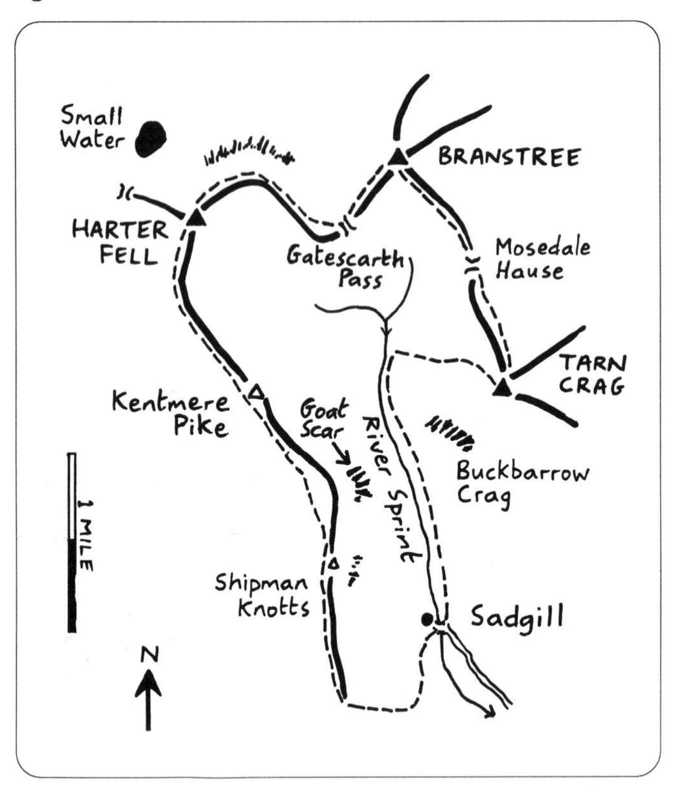

Branstree

Branstree is the large grassy dome to the north, and the first move thereto is to make acquaintance with the fence running within 300 yards of Tarn Crag's cairn, to the north-east. It runs unfailingly down to the peaty depression of Mosedale Hause, across which its left side is best followed up the unexciting slope of Branstree. Soon a wall takes over, and with it the gradient slowly but surely eases until the extensive top of Branstree is mounted. The highest point is found just a few yards beyond the wall's abrupt terminus at another fence.

Harter Fell

Branstree and Harter Fell are linked by a fence that renders the walk between them foolproof. Heading left (south-west) from the wall-end it descends without ado to the top of Gatescarth Pass, from where a much trodden path commences an immediate climb of Harter Fell. Cutting out the steep little pull to Adam Seat, the path slants across to rejoin the fence for a simple rise above the fell's increasingly craggy northern face. At a sharp angle of the fence a cairn marks a magnificent viewpoint for Mardale - the best on this walk - before the final stroll along to the wrought-iron embellished summit cairn.

For the return to Sadgill faith is retained in the fence as it heads south over the broad spine of the mountain. A short drop to a double depression precedes an equally short climb, now with a wall, to the summit of Kentmere Pike; an Ordnance column is found just over the wall. The path continues south-east, soon short-cutting the fence which runs out towards the top of Goat Scar, a splendid Longsleddale viewpoint. The main path heads for a prominent stile in another wall before the gentle rise onto Shipman Knotts. This minor top is also split by a wall, with a tiny cairn on its east side.

From here on the path finally gets to grips with the descent, a wholly enjoyable business which ultimately brings arrival at the highest point of the Stile End track linking Sadgill with Kentmere. Turning left, it remains level for a short while before concluding with a most pleasant finale, passing below Sadgill Woods before completing the walk at the shapely bridge.

LOG OF THE WALKS

WALK	DATE	TIME		WEATHER	COMMENTS
		Start	Finish		
1					
2					
3					
4					
5					
6					
7					
8					
9					
10					
11					

13					
14					
15					
16					
17					
18					
19					
20					
21					
22					
23					
24					
25					

HILLSIDE GUIDES

LONG DISTANCE WALKS - LAKE DISTRICT

1 * **THE WESTMORLAND WAY** Appleby to Arnside
2 * **THE FURNESS WAY** Arnside to Ravenglass
3 * **THE CUMBERLAND WAY** Ravenglass to Appleby

LONG DISTANCE WALKS - NORTHERN ENGLAND

7 * **CLEVELAND WAY COMPANION** Helmsley to Filey
9 * **NORTH BOWLAND TRAVERSE** Slaidburn to Stainforth (by David Johnson)
16 * **DALES WAY COMPANION** Ilkley to Bowness

CIRCULAR WALKS - YORKSHIRE DALES

4 * **WALKS IN WHARFEDALE**
5 * **WALKS IN NIDDERDALE**
6 * **WALKS IN THE CRAVEN DALES**
8 * **WALKS IN WENSLEYDALE**
10 * **WALKS IN THE WESTERN DALES**
11 * **WALKS IN SWALEDALE**

CIRCULAR WALKS - NORTH YORK MOORS

13 * **WESTERN** - The Cleveland and Hambleton Hills
14 * **SOUTHERN** - Rosedale/Farndale/Bransdale
15 * **NORTHERN** - Eskdale and the Coast

CIRCULAR WALKS - SOUTH PENNINES

12 * **WALKS IN BRONTE COUNTRY** - around Haworth
17 * **WALKS IN CALDERDALE** - around Hebden Bridge

HILLWALKING - THE LAKE DISTRICT

18 * **OVER LAKELAND MOUNTAINS** - above 2000 feet
19 * **OVER LAKELAND FELLS** - below 2000 feet

By the same author, published by Cordee, Leicester:

80 DALES WALKS - A hardback omnibus edition of Books 4, 6, 8, 10 and 11.

COMPANION TO THIS VOLUME

OVER LAKELAND FELLS

30 Half-day Fellwalks below 2000 ft

by

Paul Hannon

Ard Crags from Rigg Beck

Designed for those plentiful Lakeland days when either the high tops are shrouded in mist, or one is simply not quite up to a major expedition.

In this book, old favourites such as Catbells and Haystacks will be found alongside less frequented but equally colourful hills such as Steel Knotts and Sale Fell.

ISBN 1 870141 10 5

HILLSIDE PUBLICATIONS